Baseball and Country Music

A RAY AND PAT BROWNE BOOK

Series Editors
Ray B. Browne and Pat Browne

Baseball and Country Music

Don Cusic

THE UNIVERSITY OF WISCONSIN PRESS

THE POPULAR PRESS

The University of Wisconsin Press
1930 Monroe Street
Madison, Wisconsin 53711

www.wisc.edu/wisconsinpress/

3 Henrietta Street
London WC2E 8LU, England

1   3   5   4   2

Printed in the United States of America

Library of Congress Cataloging-in-Publication Data
Cusic, Don.
Baseball and country music / Don Cusic.
p.   cm.—(A Ray and Pat Browne book)
Includes bibliographical references.
ISBN 0-87972-857-4 (hardcover: alk. paper)
ISBN 0-87972-858-2 (pbk.: alk. paper)
1. Baseball—Social aspects—United States—History.
2. Country music—United States—History.
3. Popular culture—United States.
I. Title.   II. Series.
GV867.64.C87   2003
796.357′0973—dc21   2003007235

Contents

Contents

Baseball and Country Music

Introduction

The story of baseball tells us a lot about America, and so does the story of country music. Each is supremely American, and each presents a unique history of America, particularly during the twentieth century. In the preface to the book *Baseball: An Illustrated History*, Ken Burns and Lynn Novick write, "The story of baseball is also the story of race in America, of immigration and assimilation; of the struggle between labor and management, of popular culture and advertising, of myth and the nature of heroes, villains, and buffoons; of the role of women and class and wealth in our society."[1] The same could be said for country music.

In terms of "race," the story of baseball is part of the story of civil rights, beginning with the segregation of baseball before 1947, the creation of the Negro leagues and rise of black baseball stars, and then the introduction of Jackie Robinson to the major leagues. For country music the story is not so clear; country music has never really been integrated to any great extent, but it doesn't bar African Americans from its ranks either. Nashville as a city played an important part in the civil rights story in the 1960s and 1970s and was the scene of some of the earliest downtown lunch counter sit-ins, the starting point for some of the Freedom Riders, home of Fisk University, and home of James Lawson, who showed Martin Luther King Jr. and other civil rights leaders how to implement nonviolent resistance.

But the country music community was a world apart—just like whites and blacks lived worlds apart before the 1960s, and still do today to a large extent. In 1968 many in country music supported George Wallace for president and admired his stand for "segregation today, segregation tomorrow, segregation forever" in the South. And yet country music's black superstar, Charley Pride, also emerged during this same period. Interestingly, Charley Pride had been a baseball player in the Negro leagues and even had a tryout with the California Angels and first went to Nashville after failing to get a tryout at the New York Mets spring training camp. Although most of the audience for country music was opposed to integration, a number of key people in the country music community supported Charley Pride and gave him the chance to become a country music superstar.

The story of immigration and assimilation in baseball comes from European immigrants, particularly those from Ireland and Germany, who found in baseball a way to fulfill the American dream. The Irish brought fiddle tunes and other music that would be a foundation for contemporary commercial country music. The Germans introduced the beer hall and dances that would evolve in country music dance clubs, the two-step and line dancing.

The struggle between labor and management in baseball is the struggle of autocratic owners who kept contractual control over baseball players' careers through the "reserve" clause, which was interpreted by the owners to mean a lifetime bondage to one team, until Marvin Miller, executive director of the Major League Players Association, came along and helped break that hold. For country music there hasn't been that kind of conflict, although record companies and artists are always locked in a struggle of entertainment versus business. The recording contract has its faults and drawbacks, but country artists have generally felt that the benefits outweighed the disadvantages in these contracts, which always favor the recording companies. Popular culture is based on an open market capitalist economy, and country music has profited from this; because it has sold so well it has been recorded and made available to the American public. This has happened in spite of the scorn and derision that many New York and Los Angeles executives have heaped on the music; but they saw the dollar signs and just ignored the music.

In terms of advertising we must look at the influence the media has had on baseball and country music. Every recording and every baseball game are, essentially, advertisements, but because they are also entertainment they are given time in the media. The growth of radio and television has ensured that each received national coverage as the twentieth century progressed.

In terms of advancing the role of women, country music has done much better than baseball. Professional baseball only allowed women's leagues to form during and immediately after World War II, when it was feared that men's leagues would fold because of the wartime draft. But baseball as a whole has excluded women. Not so with country music. Many women have become country music stars, and by the 1990s around 65 percent of all country music recordings were purchased by women. The female country music stars—Kitty Wells, Patsy Cline, Loretta Lynn, Tammy Wynette, Reba McEntire—have spoken to the public from the woman's point of view, and this has been a key to their success. Even in the executive ranks there has been a number of successful women—something that certainly cannot be said of baseball.

The story of class and wealth in American society is a touchy one, because Americans generally refuse to admit to living in a class-based society. But the simple fact remains that baseball and country music both have their roots in the white working class and early on were looked down on by the upper classes and considered entertainment for roughs and rowdies, the great unwashed masses. Both have fought against this stereotype and become the sport and music of the middle class. In Nashville the city fathers intensely disliked the image of country music taking over "the Athens of the South" image they had carefully and assiduously cultivated. Upper-crust Nashville saw itself as a bastion of high culture, and country music shattered that image. Still, the city's elite managed to keep those in country music on the outside of "respected" society—that is, until money changed everything. Country music and musicians made too much money for the elite to ignore them.

Also, the many executives in both country music and baseball desired acceptance and social standing and worked hard to obtain it. Their success in business made them legitimate in the eyes of more traditional businessmen, even when the traditional businessmen didn't quite understand the business of baseball or country music. As baseball and country music proved themselves to be profitable businesses, social acceptance soon followed. The same could not be said for the players and performers, however, who often came out of the working class and who generally had no social ambition. Their lives revolved around their profession, and when they left their profession, they returned to their working-class roots. For those players and performers in the early years who did aspire to join the ranks of high society it was a long, uphill struggle, and most never did quite fit in.

Finally, there is the notion of the hero. There is no doubt that many children look up to and emulate baseball players and country music stars, who always appear larger than life. And there is no doubt that the accomplishments of baseball players and country music artists touch the lives of their followers, many of whom invest much of their lives following the exploits of these heroes. Adult fans, too, are touched by these players and performers who reflect, or articulate, their own dreams and aspirations. Country artists often express the thoughts and feelings of their fans through lyrics in their songs, while baseball players keep their fans in touch with the child deep inside each adult.

One country music group was actually formed because the two founding members shared heroes in baseball and country music. Doug Green and Fred LaBour lived next door to each other in Nashville; one day Fred saw Doug in the yard throwing a baseball and joined him in a game of pitch-and-catch. They discovered that they had both grown up in Michigan loving the Tigers, especially Al Kaline. This led to them playing on a softball team together. They also discovered that they both loved the singing cowboys—the Sons of the Pioneers, Gene Autry, and Roy Rogers—and this led to the formation of their own country music group, Riders in the Sky.

Each summer during Country Music's Fan Fair in Nashville there is a celebrity softball game. While there is a big gap between the games of softball and baseball, the differences become insignificant when fans watch country stars playing a version of the national past time. In 1997 Nolan Ryan came in as a guest celebrity and pitched; his catcher was Billy Ray Cyrus, who went to college on baseball scholarships and was intent on becoming the next Johnny Bench before he gave up baseball for a career on the stage singing. Country stars, both male and female, play the game. As shown by this softball game, what baseball and country music have most in common is the ability to provide entertainment for their fans. They touch the lives of the many who sing only in the shower or watch baseball only from an armchair but nonetheless find in country music artists and baseball players something that transcends the ordinary and takes those born without wealth, privilege, or social status and turns them into heroes by virtue of their natural talents, dedication, and hard work. In other words, both baseball and country music are tickets to the American Dream.

I

The Early Years

In April 1861, when the first shots of the Civil War were fired at Fort Sumter, South Carolina, the seeds for baseball and country music had already been firmly planted. What evolved into commercial country music songs were minstrel songs, which were performed in blackface by itinerant entertainers, and British and European folk songs, which were sung primarily in the South and whose tunes and melodic structure were the basis for the minstrel songs. The first "country" songwriter, Stephen Foster, had successfully turned out songs such as "Oh, Susannah," "Old Folks at Home," and "My Old Kentucky Home" by this time, although he would die in 1864, just before the Civil War ended. The seeds of baseball grew out of the English games of cricket and rounders, and the game had already developed into something uniquely American, first through baseball clubs in New York and then as an informal field sport throughout the rest of the country. At this point what linked country music and baseball, and would continue to for the next century, was that they served as entertainment for white, working-class Americans. The upper classes and "respectable" middle class shunned the somewhat disreputable entertainment of the lower, working class.

Like country music, baseball drew many of its early participants from the blue-collar class. According to Edward G. White in his book *Creating the National Pastime: Baseball Transforms Itself 1903–1953,* "Baseball had started in America as a working-class sport, played by Irish, German, and British immigrants in large cities. Its early history included close connections with gambling, drinking, and general rowdiness. Its early owners were not, for the most part, representatives of the well-born classes, but entrepreneurs seeking upward mobility and public recognition."[1]

The first minstrel groups were the Virginia Minstrels, formed in early 1843 in New York and led by Daniel Emmett, who would write "Dixie," and E. P. Christy's Minstrels, formed in 1844, who popularized Stephen Foster's songs. These minstrel shows evolved into varieties and then vaudeville, both of which had reputations as unsavory as that of early baseball. The early shows were aimed primarily at men and were generally held in saloons and theaters. Pickpockets, con artists, and hustlers often followed vaudeville shows and fleeced audiences, until the "family" show was developed by Tony Pastor, then Edward Albee and B. F. Keith, at the end of the nineteenth century.

Although neither the minstrel shows nor vaudeville contained "country" music as it is known today, both used songs and tunes based on the British folk-song melodies and written for the stage. The performers generally came from the working-class white population and, like early baseball, survived by attracting people with raw natural talent who saw this field as a way to make a good living outside manual labor. The upper classes preferred high culture, which included classical music and opera, and discouraged its members from participating in such low-class activities as professional sports or entertainment aimed at the masses.

The "look" of baseball players and country performers was also established just after the Civil War. For baseball it was player-captain Harry Wright, who in 1868 served as head of the Cincinnati Base Ball Club, which is generally recognized as the first all-professional team. Wright "permanently altered baseball attire when he had his men abandon the pantaloons players everywhere had worn up to then, in favor of flannel knickers and woolen stockings. Combined with jockey-style caps . . . and half-sleeved flannel blouses with soft collars, the Cincinnati garb established the basic elements of the baseball uniform that would still be worn a century later."[2] The country performer's look was developed in vaudeville and consisted of bib overalls and, often, some blacked-out teeth, suggesting the image that would still appear a century later on the TV program *Hee Haw*. Vaudeville increasingly stereotyped "country" people as rubes and hayseeds, and this image continued to be part of country music and was even used by the musicians. Performers in the early years affected the mountaineer image until that of the cowboy began to take over during the 1930s following the popularity of singing cowboys in the movies.[3]

In the *business* of baseball and country music, nineteenth-century entrepreneurs organized sporting and live musical events for paying customers. The businessmen who organized events promoted them to the community, invested in performers and players, and then made a profit if enough paying customers came. The future success of these businessmen depended on customers feeling they received their money's worth and who would then spread the word to other potential customers, which ensured the promoter of a ready audience.

However, even though these baseball games and musical concerts were *business* ventures to the performers and entrepreneurs within the field, to the audience they were *entertainment,* and the "performances" had a meaning beyond mere commerce. According to Edward White, "baseball was thought of as a business, a form of entertainment for profit, but was implicitly presented as a much more engaging spectacle than a circus or an opera or a play. It conjured up idyllic rural and pastoral associations, although staged in an urban setting."[4] Musical performances of early country music also transported the audiences, and fans attached themselves to these performers.

Still, it was the *business* of it all that allowed these entertainments to thrive. Once businessmen became involved and sought to market their "product," players and performers were paid and thus became professionals, the implication being that a professional ballplayer or a professional entertainer had achieved a level of ability beyond the ordinary. Thus audiences were not just seeing entertainment but were watching talented individuals who transcended the amateur, and so the aesthetic of the game or show was elevated. Future success also depended on the recruitment, and development, of talented people and on making these players and performers full-timers in their field thereby distinguishing them from amateurs who saw baseball and country music as merely part-time avocations or hobbies.

The media that linked the two ventures was print, in particular the newspaper. Since sports and music were both business venture and popular entertainment, the businessmen involved in sports and entertainment took out advertisements to attract customers, and the newspapers wrote stories about these events to satisfy their readers' demands. This coverage attracted readers who purchased newspapers in order to keep up with the games, concerts, players, and performers in their area. This business of entertainment was good business for newspapers, too. Out of these business concerns, newspapers developed the sports section and the entertainment sections.

By the 1920s baseball had developed into a national sport and was organized into two leagues, the American and National. Although Organized Baseball, as it was officially known, had no teams further west than St. Louis or further south than Washington, the Pacific Coast League was thriving on the West Coast, and in the South there were a number of semi-professional teams. By 1920 baseball as a business was far ahead of country music, although because of radio and recordings that would change a great deal over the next two decades.

. A key link between baseball and country music during the 1920s was radio. Both depended on radio for attracting local audiences of paying customers for the live show or game, as well as eventually a national audience.

Baseball hit the airwaves first. Shortly after the nation's first commercial station, KDKA in Pittsburgh, went on the air on November 2, 1920, it broadcast a baseball game. The date was August 5, 1921, and the place was Forbes Field, where the Pirates and Phillies played. The game was broadcast by Harold Arlin, who worked for Westinghouse, which owned the station. Also in 1921 was the broadcast of the first World Series. At this time the Series was a best-of-nine-game event, but only the first game, announced by *New York Herald Tribune* reporter Grantland Rice, was broadcast.

That game was held at the Polo Grounds, and the Yankees beat the Giants 3–0. (In an interesting connection, Grantland Rice was born in Murfreesboro, Tennessee, about forty miles from downtown Nashville, and went to college at Vanderbilt. He began his career as a sportswriter in Nashville, where the baseball park was only a few blocks away from the National Life and Accident Insurance Company, which would found radio station WSM and the Grand Ole Opry in the 1920s.)

In 1922 the entire nine-game World Series was broadcast. It was a repeat of the Yankees-Giants rivalry, and once again Grantland Rice announced the game, this time joined by writer W. B. McGheehan and engineer Raymond F. Guy. The first World Series broadcast carried nationwide, courtesy of a "network" of broadcasts beamed from radio tower to radio tower across the country, occurred in 1923, with Grantland Rice and Graham McNamee announcing. During that series Rice left the broadcast booth after the fourth inning of game three because he was bored, so it was McNamee who called the Giants-Yankees match-up that saw Babe Ruth hit three homers, Bob Meusel bat in eight runs, Frankie Frisch's stellar play in the field and .400 Series average, and Casey Stengel's inside-the-park home run as the Giants beat the Yankees four games to two. This was the first season for Yankee Stadium and the first broadcasts from "the house that Ruth built."

By 1922 WSB in Atlanta was featuring country performers in their broadcasts, the most famous of which was Fiddlin' John Carson, whose 1923 recording of "Little Old Log Cabin in the Lane" backed with "The Old Hen Cackled and the Rooster's Gonna Crow" essentially began the commercial country music recording industry. By the end of 1922 there were 510 radio stations licensed for the airwaves. In January 1923 a square dance began at WBAP in Fort Worth, Texas, led by fiddler M. J. Bonner, and sometime around 1925 WBAP began carrying a regular Friday-night barn dance. The term *barn dance* was used to identify a "rural" or "country" music radio show. Meanwhile, in Chicago at WLS, a station owned by Sears, Roebuck and Co., a barn dance began on April 19, 1924, and was held at the Sherman Hotel. The official beginning of *The WSM Barn Dance* in Nashville was November 28, 1925, when George D. Hay, who created the original show, hosted fiddler Uncle Jimmy Thompson. *The WSM Barn Dance* changed its name to *The Grand Ole Opry* in 1927.

In 1928 Prairie Farmer Publications purchased WLS from Sears, and the station increased its wattage from 500 to 5,000 watts. In 1931 it received a license for a 50,000-watt clear-channel signal and in March 1932 moved to the Eighth Street Theater in Chicago. This geographically central location and clear-channel wattage made the WLS show the first national barn dance. In September 1933 *The National Barn Dance* from WLS went over the NBC network and was sponsored by Miles Laboratories, makers of Alka-Seltzer.

In Nashville WSM also received a clear-channel 50,000-watt license in 1932, which gave *The Grand Ole Opry* a larger audience. Meanwhile, in Des Moines *The Iowa Barn Dance Frolic* began in 1932; in Charlotte, North Carolina, *The Crazy Barn Dance,* sponsored by the Texas-based laxative company Crazy Water Crystals, began in 1934; and in Knoxville *The Mid-Day Merry-Go-Round* began over WNOX in 1936 and, later, the Saturday-night show *WNOX Carnival* began, which was later renamed *Tennessee Barn Dance*.

The World's Original WWVA Jamboree in Wheeling, West Virginia, began in 1933, and it was broadcast over another 50,000-watt clear-channel station. In 1937 John Lair left WLS in Chicago and began a barn dance over WLW in Cincinnati; this *Renfroe Valley Barn Dance* moved to the Renfroe Valley location in Rockcastle County, Kentucky, on November 4, 1939. Lair, with performers Whitey Ford and Red Foley, broadcast over the Mutual Network. In 1939 WLW began *Boone County Jamboree* while *Renfro Valley Barn Dance* shifted to WHAS in Louisville, where it was carried over the CBS network.

Chicago was a center for radio broadcasts of both country music and baseball during the 1920s. Cubs owner William Wrigley liked to use radio broadcasts to promote his chewing gum company as well as his Cubs team. In 1925 the White Sox and Cubs had all their home games broadcast by Hal Totten over WMAQ, which was owned by the *Chicago Daily News*. That same year WGN began broadcasting games with announcer Quin Ryan. Cubs first baseman Charlie "Jolly Cholly" Grimm played for the team from 1925 to 1936 and then began broadcasting Cubs games on WGN.

Because of the successful marriage of radio and baseball in Chicago, other cities soon followed suit. In Philadelphia, home of the Athletics and Phillies, games were called by broadcaster Bill Dyer. In St. Louis, home of the Cardinals and Browns, baseball games were broadcast beginning in 1927, the same year broadcasts began for the Detroit Tigers. In Boston, home of the Red Sox and Braves, games were broadcast beginning in 1925, which also saw the beginning of the broadcasting of Cleveland Indians games. The Cincinnati Reds games were broadcast from Crosley Field beginning in 1929.

Since Chicago is centrally located, and since AM radio's signal can be broadcast in all directions, it is natural that Chicago had the biggest advantage of any American city in terms of radio. In addition to being the second-largest city in the United States during the 1920s, broadcasts from Chicago could be beamed in any direction and find an audience.

Both baseball and country music benefited from national stars who emerged during the 1920s. For baseball it was Babe Ruth and his home runs; for country music it was Jimmie Rodgers and his blue yodels. Two key executives emerged from these fields at this time: baseball commissioner Judge Kenesaw Mountain Landis and record producer and publisher Ralph Peer.

Babe Ruth, a left-handed pitcher for the Boston Red Sox, joined the Yankees in 1920. Ruth's hitting skills soon led to him becoming an everyday player in the outfield. During his first year with the Yankees, Ruth hit .376 with 137 runs batted in and 54 home runs—more home runs than any other *team* hit except for the St. Louis Browns. The dead ball era was over and the long ball era had begun. But Babe Ruth was more than just a great hitter. Fans loved not only his towering home runs but this outgoing, exuberant, devil-may-care attitude as well. Kids made him their hero as he became a national figure both on and off the field, leading the New York Yankees to become the dominant team in baseball throughout the 1920s.

Ruth's emergence as a baseball hero came at a critical time in the history of the sport. In 1919 the infamous Black Sox scandal occurred when a number of White Sox players made deals with gamblers to throw the World Series against the Cincinnati Reds. The case did not come to court until the following year—the Babe's first with New York—and players were eventually found not-guilty, although a Philadelphia newspaper had published an article that stated the game had been "fixed." At this point the baseball owners realized that

their sport as well as their livelihood were in danger—
If baseball was fixed why bother to watch? And if baseball was infested with gamblers who controlled the
game, then it could not be family entertainment and
certainly was not fit for young boys. So they hired a
commissioner to oversee the game. Because the owners
were in such desperate straits, the man they chose,
Judge Kenesaw Mountain Landis, a federal judge from
Chicago, assumed a lot of power the owners normally
would have been reluctant to give up.

Landis was an autocratic ruler, and many can fault
his imperious manner; however, he did restore integrity
to the game and ruled the sport with an iron fist until
his death in 1944. One of his first acts was to permanently bar players connected to gamblers during the
1919 World Series, including Shoeless Joe Jackson. Although in one sense it "solved" the problem of the
questionable integrity of baseball, it also cast a large
black cloud over the game.

Country music received its initial national exposure
in June 1923 when record executive Ralph Peer traveled
to Atlanta, Georgia, to record Fiddlin' John Carson.
Peer went to Atlanta at the request of record distributor
Polk Brockman, who had an important retailing ac-
count with Peer's company and who wanted the fiddler
recorded. Inspired by a film clip of a fiddling contest
sponsored by Henry Ford that he had seen in New York
while on a business trip, Polk Brockman thought the
rural audience would buy recordings of fiddling music.

Carson, a fiddling contest winner, had appeared regularly on Atlanta's radio station WSB. The year before, 1922, country fiddler Uncle Eck Robertson had gone to New York and recorded a fiddle tune, "Sally Goodin'," for Victor records, but that recording had not achieved any commercial success.

The New York recording executives, even though they felt it was bad music, placated the Atlanta distributor because it was good business. The recording of Carson fiddling and singing "Little Old Log Cabin in the Lane" on one side with "The Old Hen Cackled and the Rooster's Gonna Crow" on the other side was released without a commercial number. But the one thousand copies sent to Brockman sold quickly and the distributor ordered more; the label executives then realized they had a large potential audience of rural white southerners.

Field recordings were not feasible during the early 1920s because the heavy, bulky recording equipment could not easily be transported and set up. Still, the recording companies realized there was a market for these country songs—called folk, old-time, or hillbilly at first—so they began to record singers in the New York studios singing these songs. One singer, Vernon Dalhart, recorded "The Prisoner's Song," which was so commercially successful it outsold most "pop" records in 1926. Carson and Dalhart showed the New York recording executives that there was a lucrative market for this music. Beginning in 1926, when portable recording equipment was developed, recording professionals began traveling throughout the South making field recordings of native rural singers.

In 1927 the New York Yankees famous Murderer's Row—Babe Ruth, Lou Gehrig, Tony Lazzeri, Earle Combs, and Bob Meusel, along with pitchers Waite Hoyt, Herb Pennock, Urban Shocker, and Wilcy Moore—led their team to 110 wins (in a 154 game season) and a World Series victory over the Pirates. This was the year Babe Ruth hit sixty home runs. It was also the year that Ralph Peer spent the summer traveling in the South recording acts for Victor Records. During the first days of August in Bristol, Tennessee, Peer recorded two acts who would have a major impact on country music: Jimmie Rodgers, a tubercular singer from Ashville, North Carolina, and the Carter Family, husband and wife A. P. and Sara Carter with their sister-in-law Maybelle Carter, who came from Maces Springs, Virginia.

A number of country music historians mark these recordings as the beginning of commercial country music. Certainly the sales success of these two acts ushered in an era when New York recording labels saw the southern white working class as a significant market for recordings done by native rural acts. Also, Ralph Peer established a royalty payment system for songwriters and copyrighted a number of songs both old and new, which made the publishing of country songs lucrative for songwriters and publishers. Thus the financial structure for the business of country music was established, with the sales of recordings and the copyrights of songs proving to be good business ventures for New York executives.

The importance of the Bristol sessions extends beyond the commercial success that ensued for Victor Records, because Jimmie Rodgers became to country music what Babe Ruth was to baseball. Like Ruth, who inspired countless young boys to pick up a bat and ball, Rodgers inspired rural boys to try singing for a living. The boys who looked at Babe Ruth as a hero swung for the fence; the boys who looked at Jimmie Rodgers as a hero sang blue yodels, slipping into falsetto in key parts of the song. A generation of baseball players and country singers was influenced by these two men who led their fields into the future.

2

Radio and Electricity

At the end of the 1930s neither country music nor baseball was seeing major revenue from radio. Both were in the business of selling tickets to fans who went to the ballpark or the show. The owners were interested in attracting a crowd, and although they saw radio as a means of advertising their wares, most power brokers in country music and baseball feared that radio would "steal" their audience: if people could hear the music or listen to the game over the air for "free," they would not purchase tickets and fill the seats.

Baseball team owners recognized the importance of sports writers from local newspapers who followed the teams and wrote about the games. A daily story of a game played the previous day was a good advertisement for the games scheduled for that day and the next. Also, the newspaper coverage gave fans who could not attend the game a recap of the event. Radio, however, posed a different problem: radio broadcast the game live, as it happened. This conflict in game coverage was initially overlooked because a number of radio stations were owned by newspapers and the broadcasters were sports writers, so local stations in some major league cities—including Chicago, Boston, Cleveland, St. Louis, Philadelphia, and Detroit—were initially allowed to broadcast some home games.

There had been national broadcasts of the World Series since 1922, but with limited advertising. The big money did not arrive until 1934, when Commissioner Landis negotiated a four-year $400,000 Series sponsorship with the Ford Motor Company. Still, most owners did not see the benefits of broadcasting regular games since there was no money from broadcast rights.

Organized by a Chicago sports writer, the All-Star Game was first played in 1933 (the same year Jimmie Rodgers died). The game was so popular that it became an annual event. In 1935 the third All-Star Game was broadcast nationally over the radio. The networks paid a fee for the broadcast rights, although there were no commercials during the game. Realizing there was a large market of radio listeners for baseball games and wanting exclusive access to that market, radio stations began paying clubs for the right to broadcast home games. And since advertisers also wanted to reach a large market, it soon became obvious there was potential revenue for baseball teams to work with a particular radio station and sponsor to broadcast games. General Mills, with its Wheaties cereal, was an early and important advertiser of baseball.

Still, some cities held out. In April 1936 the New York City baseball clubs—the Yankees, Giants, and Dodgers—imposed a ban on broadcasting games. The owners claimed that if fans could hear the game on the radio, they would not come to the ballpark. And the only way the owners made money was when people came to the ballpark, purchased a ticket to enter, and then spent some extra money on a score card and food. Sponsors who paid for the rights to broadcast games did manage to change the owners' minds. Club owners were surprised to discover that not only the sponsors benefited by selling their product but the owners benefited as well, because the games themselves were an advertisement that reached a larger audience and boosted attendance. The broadcast games also reached the younger fan base who could not attend games but who would follow the team, learn about the players, and become the next generation of paying customers.

The major recording industry companies also fought radio for much the same reason baseball owners did. Network radio during the 1930s consisted of a number of live broadcasts of Big Bands that had sponsors. These bands and their leaders knew that radio appearances were lucrative because sponsors paid them and because these shows were good advertisements for live appearances. They wanted to give sponsors the exclusive advertising rights they demanded and saw recordings as an unwelcome intruder on this arrangement. After all, why would the radio stations pay the music act when they could get the recording for free? And why would fans attend a live concert as a paying customer when they could hear the recording on the radio for free?

Another factor (one that is difficult to imagine today) was that radio station personnel as a whole considered it dishonest and deceptive to broadcast shows that had been previously recorded. The prevailing idea was that audiences expected what they heard on the radio to be brought to them live in real time, so it was unethical to "deceive" the audiences by playing recorded music.

In 1940 two very important things happened that would affect country music on radio. First, the Supreme Court let stand a lower court ruling which stated that when someone purchased a recording, all property rights belonged to the buyer. This meant that when a disc jockey purchased a record he was allowed to play it on the air. While this did not protect the notion of intellectual property and, considered in the light of subsequent copyright questions, was a bad decision for the music business as a whole, it did make radio airplay for records legal. This ruling curbed the efforts of the record companies to enforce the ban on radio airplay.

The record companies Victor and Columbia were prepared to charge radio stations for their products in 1940 until the Supreme Court ruling was announced. Capitol Records, just formed at the end of 1941, took advantage of the situation and became the first label to distribute free "promotional copies" to radio stations for on-air play. Prior to this only music editors and record reviewers for print media were given free promotional recordings.[1]

Also in 1940 James Caesar Petrillo from Chicago was elected to head the American Federation of Musicians. Petrillo ruled his union firmly and campaigned vigorously to get records banned from the radio because they would displace musicians who earned their livelihood from live performances, many of which were broadcast on the radio. Petrillo announced at the American Federation of Musicians annual convention in May 1942 that he would call a strike of all musicians on August 1, 1942. Another issue Petrillo fought aggressively was the broadcast of "canned music."

The musicians' strike lasted until the end of 1944. When war broke out Petrillo did allow for an exception to be made for V-Disk records, which were shipped to armed forces personnel around the world. (This explains the V-Disk group recording its own product.) When, finally, a settlement was reached—the new contract between the record labels and the musicians' union featured better working conditions and the establishment of the Performance Trust Fund for out-of-work musicians—the record companies began recording again.

This fight against putting recordings on radio was actually led by the major labels and the Big Bands, which produced the dominant commercial music of the day. For country music, which had very limited exposure on radio, the argument was nearly moot. The country music industry actually benefited a great deal from recordings because a major outlet for this music was the jukebox, especially after Prohibition was lifted in 1933 and bars attracted the working class as customers.

The money from radio provided an important revenue stream to both baseball and the music business. At first it came from individual sponsors who paid the radio stations that broadcast the games. Then, in 1934, the sponsor paid the league for the World Series, and the money filtered down to the teams involved. For music, individual sponsors paid a radio station (or a network) an amount for the show in exchange for advertisements run during the show. In both cases the baseball team or the musical act benefited directly from the radio station's payment for their services or access and indirectly from increased exposure that resulted in more paying customers for their live shows.

The technology that benefited the live music shows the most, however, was not radio but the electric light.

People could go to a concert or performance after work, in the evenings or at night, which allowed a musical act to perform more often. When an act could only perform on weekends or during the noon hour, the audience was more limited. Also, it allowed the act to perform before larger crowds and in better conditions. What is surprising is that it took baseball so long to realize this.

Less than 5 percent of all American homes had electricity by 1910, although in the first stage of electrification in America, from roughly 1885 to 1910, a number of theaters, hotels, department stores, and nightclubs had electricity usually provided by their own electrical generator. However, during the 1920s most American homes in urban areas were wired for electricity; and by 1930 70 percent had electricity. This increased to 96 percent by 1934. By 1935 most cities and towns in the United States had electricity, although many rural areas did not. This meant that most homes in cities and towns across the country had electrical, rather than crystal, radios by the mid-1930s. It also meant that people could shop or find entertainment in the evening in stores and clubs and movie theaters lit by electrical lights.

But it was not until 1935 that major league baseball was played at night. This first game, played on May 24, 1935, between the Cincinnati Reds and the Phillies, attracted 20,422 fans. The Dodgers began playing night games in 1938 (their first night game at Ebbets Field in

Brooklyn on June 15, 1938, achieved further distinction when Reds pitcher Johnny Vander Meer hurled his second consecutive no-hitter that night). But other teams were slow to catch on; seven other clubs installed lights between 1939 and 1941, but it was not until after World War II that the Yankees, Red Sox, and Tigers played night baseball.

Night baseball had come to the minor leagues earlier; the first night game in the Southern Association was played on July 21, 1930, in Little Rock, Arkansas, and the first night game for the Nashville Vols, also a member of the Southern Association, was on May 18, 1931, against Mobile.

Both baseball and the music business are businesses driven by commercial concerns but in which noneconomic-based decisions play a large role. So while baseball saw that it could attract fans by holding games at night, there was a counterargument made that night baseball would interfere with the "purity" and "tradition" of the game. Later on country music had the same arguments against using drums or electrical instruments. Baseball and country music have always set themselves apart from everyday commerce while, at the same time, being part of it. Somehow the fans want to believe they are more than a part of a mere business transaction when they buy a ticket to a game or concert, and owners are careful to cultivate this. They foster the associations both baseball and country music have to rural America, a pastoral image connected to a time that was always more simple, pure, and honest. Kids grow up with baseball players and music stars as their heroes, and they want to be like them. This innocence and emulation are entwined with baseball and music and make these fields of dreams an important part of growing up. Roy Acuff and Eddy Arnold loved baseball but looked at Jimmie Rodgers and Gene Autry as heroes; they each began playing and singing to local audiences and on radio. Dizzy Dean and Mickey Mantle loved country music but looked to Babe Ruth and Walter Johnson as heroes; they played on community and sandlot baseball teams and then entered the minor leagues.

However, "growing up" for baseball and country music meant entering a modern era of bright lights and big cities as Americans began moving off the farms during the twentieth century.

3

Country Music and Baseball in America

Today the cities most closely associated with recorded country music are New York, Nashville, and Los Angeles. During the 1920s, however, more country music was recorded in Atlanta than any other place, though by the end of the decade Atlanta was no longer a major recording center. Many country recordings were made in New York and Newark, New Jersey, because the major label's home offices and studios were located there. Chicago also became a major center for country music because of the success of *National Barn Dance* on WLS, the first country music show broadcast on a national network. Los Angeles became a center for country music recording because that is where the singing cowboys—who were movie stars as well as recording stars—were working. It wasn't until after World

War II that Nashville began to dominate the country recording scene. Since that time Nashville has emerged as the center for the country music recording industry.

Through the first half of the twentieth century, New York and Chicago each had major league teams—the Yankees, Dodgers, and Giants in New York and the Cubs and White Sox in Chicago. And since many country artists were baseball fans, and since many baseball players came from the South, it is logical to conclude that there was some connection between the worlds of baseball and country music in New York and Chicago. However, that connection was most evident in Los Angeles and Nashville, where top minor league teams played and where a number of country artists lived.

In California baseball was first organized in San Francisco, where the Pacifics played in 1862. The first baseball league on the West Coast was the California League, which was organized in 1885 in northern California; this became known informally as the Pacific Coast League in 1898.

In September 1901 the presidents of a number of minor leagues met in Chicago where they formed the National Association of Professional Baseball Leagues in order to thwart attempts by the major leagues to raid the minor league rosters.

In 1903 there were two leagues on the West Coast: the California League and the Pacific Coast League. The Pacific Coast League proved to be more popular with teams in San Francisco, Los Angeles, Oakland,

Sacramento, Portland, and Seattle. The teams generally had rosters of fourteen to fifteen players with four pitchers expected to pitch the entire nine innings of any game they started. Since the weather was mild, the teams frequently played more than two hundred games a season, from March into late November or early December.

During the 1903 season the Los Angeles Angels was the only team in the Pacific Coast League with a winning record (133-78); their star was outfielder Gavvy Cravath, who went on to an eleven-year career in the major leagues (1908–9, 1912–20) playing for the Boston Red Sox, Chicago White Sox, Washington Senators, and Philadelphia Phillies and leading the National League in home runs for four seasons. The Angels had other future and past major league stars during their early years: first baseman Hal Chase (later caught up in the Black Sox Scandal of 1919) and Wahoo Sam Crawford, who, after his stellar nineteen-year career in the majors (and numbers good enough to get him elected to the Baseball Hall of Fame in 1957), played his last four seasons of professional baseball with Los Angeles in the Pacific Coast League.

During the 1921 season William K. Wrigley, chewing gum magnate and majority owner of the Chicago Cubs, purchased the Los Angeles Angels. This would be the only club in the Pacific Coast League that was owned by a major league club; the rest were owned independently. In 1925 the Angels moved into Wrigley Field, built by Wrigley at a cost of over a million dollars and with seating for 22,000. The Los Angeles area had another club in Vernon that moved to San Francisco and became the Missions at the end of the 1925 season. The Los Angeles area lost the Vernon team but gained a club for the next season when the Salt Lake City Bees, under owner Bill Lane, decided to move to Hollywood and become the Stars.

During the 1930s there was a great rivalry between the Los Angeles Angels and Hollywood Stars, with the Angels dominating in 1933–34. During that period San Francisco Seals center fielder Joe DiMaggio put up numbers so impressive that the New York Yankees purchased his contract. Meanwhile, in San Diego, where the Hollywood Stars moved after the 1935 season, owner Bill Lane signed a seventeen-year-old ballplayer from Herbert Hoover High School named Ted Williams.

About that same time, Gene Autry came to Hollywood to begin his movie career, arriving during the summer of 1934, when the Los Angeles Angels were the dominant team in the Pacific Coast League. Earlier that year the Sons of the Pioneers had begun recording; the group would go on to define the "western" sound through their songwriting, led by Bob Nolan, who wrote "Tumbling Tumbleweeds" and "Cool Water," and other recordings. One of the founding members, Leonard Slye, would later become known as Roy Rogers, while Gene Autry would become the first singing cowboy star and would change the image of country music from the mountaineer to the cowboy.

There was no professional baseball in Hollywood during the 1936 and 1937 seasons. However, for the 1938 season the San Francisco Missions, managed by Fred Haney, moved to Hollywood and played at Wrigley Field for one season before moving to Gilmore Field, a wooden park that seated almost 13,000 and marked the foul lines with buried pieces of wood painted white. In 1939 a local station televised a game.

The Hollywood Stars attracted a number of show business people as investors and fans; among those who owned stock in the club during its tenure were Gene Autry, Bing Crosby, Gary Cooper, Cecil B. DeMille, Barbara Stanwyck, William Powell, Robert Taylor, George Raft, George Burns, and Gracie Allen. It became the "glamour" franchise of the Pacific Coast League, which saw 2,199,270 fans attend league games in 1939. However, it was the Los Angeles Angels, not the Hollywood Stars, who won the pennant, led by former Cardinal Gashouse Gang star Rip Collins at first base.

Baseball was introduced to Nashville by Herman Sandhouse, who learned the game while attending college in Philadelphia. This game reportedly took place shortly after the end of the Civil War in north Nashville, near the present-day Fisk University.[1] The earliest published mention of a baseball game in Nashville—there called "Base Ball"—occurred in the *Nashville Dispatch,* which reported a game "between the Cumberland and Louisville Clubs" on July 31, 1866, with a crowd of "upwards of 2,000 persons" watching the game, which Louisville won 39–23.[2] The next mention of baseball was coverage of a game played on August 17, 1866, with the Cumberland Base Ball Club playing the Louisville club in Louisville with "fully five thousand people" to watch "the championship of the South." The ball game "commenced about a quarter to three" and finished with Louisville beating the Cumberland Club 72–11.[3]

Around the same time these games were played in Nashville, some students at Fisk University set out to raise money for their historically all-black school by giving concerts that featured Negro spirituals, gospel songs that had been sung by slaves. The performances were incredibly popular in the North—where audiences had seldom, if ever, heard these songs before— and the student choir even toured Europe. The result was that the Fisk Jubilee Singers not only provided the necessary income to save their university, but also gave Nashville its first strong musical identity. Indeed, until around World War II "Nashville music" was spirituals.

Baseball's first Southern League was organized in 1885 by journalist Henry W. Grady of Atlanta, who served as the league's first president. The Nashville franchise, the Volunteers, was headed by L&N Railroad official W. E. Atmore. This league disbanded in 1895. Then, in late 1900 and early 1901, the Southern League was reorganized by Abner Powell of the New Orleans club, Charley Frank of the Memphis club, and Newton Fisher of the Nashville Vols. The first season for the new league was 1901, and the first cities to have teams in the league were Birmingham, Chattanooga, Little Rock, Shreveport, Selma, New Orleans, Memphis, and Nashville. The organizers tried to get a team going in Atlanta, but there were no takers; so Selma was offered a team and took it. The league got off to a shaky start. The first league president "defaulted with all the available cash on hand" and the league was left in a precarious position.[4] In the second year Judge William Kavanaugh of Little Rock took the job and performed it well, putting the league on a solid footing. Atlanta decided to join the league, replacing Selma, and Montgomery also joined the league, replacing Chattanooga.

Some of the first baseball "owners" were railroad companies, whose responsibilities included paying the twelve players on the club and building a ballpark. The financial incentive was that people would buy tickets on the train to go to the ballpark, which was always located near the center of the city; thus, the railway line would make a profit. Some of the oldest ballparks could seat 2,000, but in the early 1900s ballparks began being built that could seat 5,000 to 8,000 fans, and on big days (like holidays) there might be as many as 10,000 watching the game. In an article written in 1910 Grantland Rice noted that "Nashville has drawn as many as 11,700 paid admissions to one game. Atlanta upon several occasions has ranged above 10,000."[5]

The Nashville Vols won the Southern League pennant in 1916; however, between 1917 and 1939 they suffered through poor teams. Things turned around when Larry Gilbert, a former member of the Boston Braves, which won the 1914 World Series, and later the manager of the New Orleans baseball club, took over as manager and part-owner of the Nashville Vols for the 1939 season.

The year 1939 was significant not only for baseball in Nashville but for the country music scene there as well. On January 7, 1939, Nashville took an important step on its journey to becoming "Music City U.S.A." when William Esty Agency advertising executive Dick Marvin convinced R. J. Reynolds executives that *The Grand Ole Opry* would be a good place to advertise their Prince Albert brand of tobacco. A loose tobacco sold in cans, Prince Albert was used for pipes or "roll-your-own" cigarettes; it was an inexpensive brand aimed at the blue-collar, working class.

Opry performers that evening, who performed fifteen-minute segments, included the Golden West Cowboys, Uncle Dave Macon, Roy Acuff, Jack and the Missouri Mountaineers, Sam and Kirk McGee, De-Ford Bailey, the Andrew Brothers, Zeke Clements, the Possum Hunters, Ford Rush, the Fruit Jar Drinkers, the Crook Brothers, and Slim Smith. They performed at the Dixie Tabernacle, an open-air pavilion on Fatherland Street, just across the Cumberland River from the courthouse. (It was not the best venue for performers;

in cold weather it was too cold and in hot weather it was too hot.) George D. Hay, the "Solemn Old Judge," ran each show, acting as talent organizer, master of ceremonies, and general power to be reckoned with. That unseasonably balmy January night he was blessed with clear skies and temperatures in the low fifties and upper forties at show time. This sponsor would provide the means for *The Grand Ole Opry* to be on the NBC network later that year, giving the show national exposure.

By this time *The Grand Ole Opry* was widely recognized as one of the most important country music shows in the nation, primarily because the WSM signal could reach so far. Also, the Opry had been attracting top-notch talent to its weekly show. Hay had organized groups such as the Fruit Jar Drinkers and the Gully Jumpers, combined or renamed existing groups, and insisted the acts perpetuate the image of mountaineers that came out of the vaudeville tradition. Evident in early photographs of Opry casts, the original Opry performers generally wore suits and ties; Hay, however, insisted that his Opry performers wear bib overalls and sit amid bales of hay in order to present a "country" image. The Opry actively promoted the idea that this was a rural-based show meant for plain country folks. Even Dr. Humphrey Bate, a physician who had graduated from Vanderbilt, changed the name of his group to the Possum Hunters and traded his suit and tie for the hillbilly look.[6]

The power structure at WSM and *The Grand Ole Opry* was beginning to change in 1939. Judge Hay suffered from depression and was increasingly losing his power, although he still ran the Opry's Saturday-night performances. Harry Stone, who had served as Hay's assistant, would take over the supervisory executive position and executive Jack Stapp would move from CBS in New York to WSM (an NBC affiliate) in Nashville to take over as head of programming for WSM. Stapp went on to create a number of successful programs, such as *Sunday Down South,* that were broadcast nationally and served to strengthen WSM's and Nashville's ties to network radio.

As changes were occurring at WSM and the Opry in the spring and summer of 1939, the Nashville Vols were offering an exciting brand of baseball at the Sulphur Dell ballpark just a few blocks north of WSM's offices. The Sulphur Dell was located three blocks northeast of the state capitol, situated between Fourth and Fifth Avenues on the east and west, Jackson Street on the north, and a spur railroad track on the south. The location had first served as a ballpark in 1885 and was built on Sulphur Springs; it was later known as Sulphur Springs Bottom and then as Athletic Park. In 1908 it was first called Sulphur Dell by Nashville sportswriter Grantland Rice, who, according to former *Nashville Banner* sportswriter Fred Russell, "often began his stories with a couplet, or a four-line verse. It was much easier for him to find a word that rhymed with Dell than one that rhymed with Bottom."[7] The ballpark was made of wood until the 1927 season, when a steel and concrete grandstand was built; at this point the diamond was moved around creating a field that had the right field fence 262 feet away. During that season Jim Poole hit fifty home runs for the Vols and teammate Jay Partridge hit forty. The main entrance was then on Fifth Avenue. After the 1930 season, when the Vols hit 157 home runs, a fifty-foot screen was put on top of the right field fence. The wooden stand seating fans for the Sulphur Dell was at the corner of Fourth and Jackson with home plate facing the state capitol. The Dell could seat about 7,800 people, and the field was twenty-two feet below street level—which was especially difficult for play in right field, where there was a sharp incline up to the fence, causing players to refer to Sulphur Dell as "Suffer Hell."

Those in and around Nashville saw baseball and *The Grand Ole Opry* as important sources of entertainment; in fact, the baseball team got much more coverage in the local newspapers than country music did! And not limiting themselves to music sponsorship, the tobacco companies, including R. J. Reynolds, got in on the act and began using baseball as an advertising venue, putting up prominent signs in the outfield and featuring their products on baseball cards and in the national media with the endorsement of baseball players. Part of the image of baseball was that of players with a bulging cheek where they kept their chaw of tobacco.

During the summer of 1939 the Vols played some exciting baseball, finishing third in the Southern League and winning the Shaughnessy Playoff by defeating Memphis and Atlanta and then the Dixie Series when they beat Fort Worth. (The Pacific League also adopted a Shaughnessy Playoff system where the teams that finished first and fourth in the league would play each other, while the teams that finished second and third would also play each other, with the winners of those two games playing for the championship.)

The nation at large was experiencing some exciting times as it was moving out of the Great Depression. At the New York World's Fair people could see "The World of Tomorrow" with bright lights everywhere and the first demonstration of a new invention called television. In Nashville the Tennessee Valley Authority had been ruled constitutional by the Supreme Court after being challenged by private utility companies that argued the government should not be involved in private business. The TVA brought cheap electricity to Nashville and the South and played a major role in the economy of the South, helping it catch up economically with the rest of the nation.

Also in 1939 the Baseball Hall of Fame opened in Cooperstown, New York. The roots of the Hall of Fame go to the Great Depression and the efforts of baseball executives and Cooperstown officials to raise money. And the roots of Cooperstown as the site extend back to Albert G. Spalding, who decided to "create" a history of baseball. Spalding had been a professional baseball player since the late-1860s, when he was the seventeen-year-old star pitcher in Chicago who worked at a wholesale grocer that arranged his hours so he could play baseball for their team. In 1874 Spalding was one of the players on a baseball team that played in Great Britain to promote the American game. After the 1877 season Spalding retired, bought stock in the Chicago White Stockings (later White Sox) baseball club, and opened a sporting goods "emporium." Spalding made an exclusive agreement with the major league teams to sell them balls for their games, and thus the Spalding empire was born.

Spalding also published *Spalding's Official Base Ball Guide,* which listed the official statistics for baseball. The editor of *Spalding's Base Ball Guide* was Henry Chadwick, the first baseball writer, who "always maintained that the American game of baseball, however distinctive it may have become, derived from the English game of rounders." But A. G. Spalding "had become so convinced that the game embodied American values and virtues that he set out to prove its indigenous origins." A special seven-man panel was created in 1905 to determine the history of baseball; their conclusion was that in 1839 in Cooperstown, New York, Abner Doubleday showed "boys a diagram for a game of 'base ball' and explained its rules." This conclusion about the origin of baseball was based on a letter from Abner Graves, a schoolmate of Doubleday's who was then a mining engineer in Denver and who was supposedly one of the boys with Doubleday that eventful day. However, according to baseball historian Charles Alexander, "at that time . . . the twenty-year-old Doubleday was already more than one hundred miles away at West Point, in his second year as a cadet at the U.S. Military Academy." Alexander observes further that "when he died in 1893, Doubleday was known for his distinguished record as a Union officer in the Civil War and as a postwar promoter of street railways. He left no record of having ever played baseball." These facts were never investigated; after all, Abner Doubleday was a genuine Civil War hero, and the "Doubleday myth quickly became a staple of American folklore, as well as what most people took for authenticated history."[8] All that mattered was that A. G. Spalding liked the story and published it as the "official" beginning of baseball. And that was how Cooperstown, New York, and baseball were forever linked.

In early May 1935 Cooperstown resident Alexander Cleland noticed that Doubleday Field, "where baseball could have been invented if only all of those other people hadn't invented it first," was being improved through one of Roosevelt's WPA projects. Cleland was an employee of the Clark Foundation, based in Cooperstown and founded by Edward S. Clark, who was business partner with Isaac Singer and who had been the business brains of the Singer Sewing Machine Company. Cleland didn't know anything about baseball but knew that a lot of people liked it and that there was some connection to Cooperstown. So Cleland thought of the idea of a baseball museum as a tourist attraction for Cooperstown and presented the idea to Stephen Clark, director of the Clark Foundation. Clark liked the idea, so he and Cleland enlisted the support of the civic leaders of Cooperstown (the Clark Foundation had already built the Fenimore House and the Farmer's Museum). Clark and Cleland also thought they needed the support of official baseball, so they contacted National League president Ford Frick in New York. By coincidence, Frick had visited the National Hall of Fame at New York University a few days before Cleland and Clark visited him, and Frick had been "much impressed, and had a notion that a Baseball Hall of Fame would be great for the game."[9]

Cleland's idea was the right one at the right time. There had already been plans to build a baseball monument in Washington, D.C., on the Potomac, that would list the names of the greatest players, but Congress had not come up with the money. The Clark Foundation would provide the funding for the museum and the hall of fame, so the problem of where to find the seed money for the venture was solved.

The first players in the Hall of Fame were elected by the Baseball Writers of America in 1936: Ty Cobb, Honus Wagner, Babe Ruth, Christy Mathewson, and

Walter Johnson. In 1937 eight more were elected, including Napoleon Lajoie, Tris Speaker, Cy Young, Connie Mack, and John McGraw. Four were elected in 1938 and nine in 1939, including Henry Chadwick, George Sisler, Willie Keeler, Charles Comiskey, Buck Ewing, and Lou Gehrig. In August 1939 the building was opened in Cooperstown and official "induction" ceremonies took place.

It wasn't until late 1958 that the Country Music Association was formed in Nashville, and one of its first ideas to promote country music and tourism was to establish a Country Music Hall of Fame, which they based on the idea of the Baseball Hall of Fame, which by 1958 was well known as both an institution and tourist attraction. An important difference between the two halls of fame, however, is the selection process. The Country Music Association has select members of their organization make the selection rather than newspaper writers. Jimmie Rodgers, along with Fred Rose and Hank Williams, was in the first group of inductees to the Country Music Hall of Fame in 1961.

4

War Clouds Gather

The Prince Albert segment of *The Grand Ole Opry* ran for nine months in 1939, during which time the Esty and R. J. Reynolds executives, pleased with the success of this promotion, decided to sponsor a thirty-minute show on the NBC "Red" network, a secondary network to NBC's major "Blue" network (the "Red" would later become ABC). It was a relatively small start: twenty-six stations across the South were to broadcast the Opry, but *The Grand Ole Opry* seemed perfect for the audience that R. J. Reynolds wanted. In fact, the Prince Albert folks would sponsor the Opry for twenty-one years, until 1960.

The National Life and Accident Insurance Company, which owned WSM, liked the Opry because its customers liked the Opry. Insurance agents for the company gave away tickets to the Opry to favored customers and prospective clients. Agents even knocked on doors and said they were with "the Grand Ole Opry Insurance Company" because it was a sure way to get into homes and sell policies.

The Opry's first network broadcast performance was held at War Memorial Auditorium, just across Seventh Avenue from the WSM offices. In July the Opry had moved from the open-air Dixie Tabernacle because of the problems the hot and cold weather presented for the performers and audiences and because it was difficult to control the crowds.

The first show was a bit rough and ragged, and so for the next week's show WSM executives Jack Stapp and Harry Stone assembled the cast on Saturday morning for a rehearsal to make sure the timing was right, that the program began and ended on the minute. The first "Prince Albert Show" from the Opry opened with Roy Acuff and his Smoky Mountain Boys singing "Having a Big Time Tonight." Then Judge Hay was introduced, and he, in turn, introduced Roy Acuff, who sang "Ida Red." Announcer David Stone followed with a commercial for Prince Albert, stating that "impartial tobacco tests" conducted at a scientific laboratory concluded that Prince Albert was "eighty-six degrees cooler" than other tobaccos, guaranteeing "smooth smoking" for "the national joy smoke." Then Uncle Dave Macon performed "Cannon County Hills." George Wilkerson and his Fruit Jar Drinkers followed with "Up Jumped the Devil," and then DeFord Bailey played "Choo Choo Blues" on his harmonica before the first of a number of congratulatory telegrams were read. The first telegram was from Tennessee governor Prentice Cooper; other telegrams came from Gene Autry, Texas governor W. Lee O' Daniel, World War I hero Alvin York, Alabama congressman Luther Patrick, and Kentucky senator Albert Chandler.

Other musical numbers performed that evening included "The Great Speckled Bird" by Roy Acuff; "Nobody's Darling but Mine" by Uncle Dave Macon; "Old Joe Clark" by the Fruit Jar Drinkers; "John Henry" by Brother Oswald and Rachael Veech; "Old Rattler" by Roy Acuff; "Away Out on the Mountain" by Uncle Dave Macon; and harmonica numbers "Fox Chase," "Evening Prayer Blues," and "Memphis Blues" by the Opry's "mascot," black performer DeFord Bailey. During the thirty-minute show there were four commercials that promoted Prince Albert; all were read by David Stone, who informed listeners that "science has determined" that Prince Albert was a "cooler" smoke that "protects against irritation and discomfort" from "excessive smoking" and that Prince Albert "rolls up easier, faster and neater" than other tobaccos. The show ended with a reminder to tune into NBC shows *Blondie* and *The Bob Crosby Orchestra* and that next Saturday night there would be Benny Goodman and the Opry.

"The Prince Albert Show" made WSM a major player in country music. Although WSM had a clear-channel 50,000-watt station that reached most of the

United States (and transcriptions were available for the West Coast), the top barn dance up to this time was considered by many to be the WLS *National Barn Dance* out of Chicago, which was a network regular before *The Grand Ole Opry* achieved that distinction. Several important things happened with the Opry because of this network connection. First, the Opry and WSM became nationally known for their country music show. Because of this they attracted national advertisers and advertising agencies that would play a major role in future national exposure. Finally, the show began to move away from the original format of the Opry show itself as the major attraction to one with a star system that promoted one act over the others. Prior to this time it was the *show* that was central and the artists were interchangeable; after this, the *star* was the central figure, although WSM and Opry executives continued to try to balance the idea that the Opry itself was essential and that's what people wanted to see and hear, versus the idea that people paid for tickets in order to see and hear a particular star. This idea of the power of an individual star shifted the balance of power in the Opry hierarchy as the show moved through the 1940s. One of the first casualties of the change was Judge Hay, who, due to the demands of the advertising agency, had to give way to Roy Acuff announcing the Prince Albert portion of the show.

The shift toward a *star* rather than the team attracting paying customers was also true in baseball. While baseball fans came to see the stars of baseball—Babe Ruth, Walter Johnson, Ty Cobb—major league baseball did not face the real drawing power of stars until the reserve clause in players' contracts was struck down in the 1970s making free agency possible. Until that time, the baseball club "owned" the player, who could not play major league baseball at all unless he was traded or sold, and kept individual player salaries low, although a few players (such as Babe Ruth) did manage to demand and receive high salaries because of their importance to the team in terms of attracting fans and winning games.

By the end of 1939 Roy Acuff was the biggest star of *The Grand Ole Opry*. Acuff was born in Maynardville, in east Tennessee, in 1903 and at sixteen moved with his family to a suburb of Knoxville. A good athlete, Acuff played baseball until he was felled by sunstroke in 1929, which forced him to spend 1930 in bed, where he learned to play his father's fiddle. In 1932 he joined a medicine show selling Mocoton Tonic (which was part alcohol), and in 1934 he was performing on WROL in Knoxville. He then moved to the *Mid-Day Merry Go Round* on station WNOX along with musicians Jess Easterday on guitar and mandolin, Clell Sumney on dobro, and Red Jones on bass. In 1935 he went back to WROL, where the group took on the name the Crazy Tennesseans.

Roy Acuff began singing "The Great Speckled Bird" on his radio show after Charlie Swain and his group, the Black Shirts, who had first popularized the song over the Knoxville radio, left town. After Acuff began performing it the song became so popular that the American Record Company (which later became Columbia Records) recorded Acuff and his group in Chicago in October 1936. Acuff had been extremely frustrated in his initial attempts to obtain an audition at WSM for the show; in October 1937 he finally got an audition, but he did not pass it. However, in February 1938, after another audition, he was hired by the Opry and made a regular member. Harry Stone insisted, however, that the name of the group be changed to the Smokey Mountain Boys, because Crazy Tennesseans seemed like a slur to the state of Tennessee. Also, he didn't want any confusion with Crazy Water Crystals, an advertiser and popular laxative. So, beginning on February 26, 1938, the group was known as Roy Acuff and the Smoky Mountain Boys.

Another baseball fan, Bill Monroe, joined the Opry in October 1939 with his group the Blue Grass Boys. Monroe went on to create bluegrass music, named after his group, and formed a baseball team made up of his band mates who, before the concerts, played exhibition games against a number of minor league teams in the South. Monroe pitched and played first base. Because he was so infatuated with baseball, Monroe often made his decisions about hiring musicians for his band with additional consideration based on how well they played ball. Banjo player Stringbean was a good pitcher, which added to his value as a musician.

Baseball was a good way to offset the rigors of touring and break up the monotony of travel. Monroe's group played six or seven nights a week and drove up to a hundred miles between shows. The Bluegrass All-Stars got some good physical exercise playing ball, and they also used the games to help promote their shows, challenging local clubs or anybody else who could put together a team. An advertisement in *Billboard* magazine in April 30, 1949, read, "Bill Monroe will carry a baseball team with him again this summer in conjunction with his personal appearance tour. Monroe intends to line up fifteen players, some of whom will double in his show, to play all comers on afternoon dates, with his show set for the evening."[1] In addition to the musicians, some of the road crew—which set up tents for Monroe's tent shows—also played. The introduction to his 1950 songbook *Bill Monroe's Blue Grass Country Songs* states that in 1949 the baseball team had an 80-50 win-loss record and that two players "were spotted by big league scouts, signed, and placed with farm clubs."[2] Later, Monroe told author Jim Rooney that if it hadn't been for his weak eyesight, "I [would] have liked to be a baseball player. I could hit good and could've been a fair player."[3]

While 1939 was an important year for both country music and baseball, the biggest news that year was taking place thousands of miles away from Nashville in Europe, where Adolf Hitler's German army had invaded Poland, forcing England and France to declare war on Germany. War clouds were gathering all over Europe, and Americans wondered where it would all lead, although the prevailing sentiment was that it was Europe's problem, and most Americans saw no reason to be involved in another foreign war.

Singing cowboy star Gene Autry toured Great Britain and Ireland in the summer of 1939. In Dublin several hundred thousand fans gathered below Autry's hotel window and sang to *him*. Among those watching this performance was Phil Wrigley, who decided to sponsor Autry on a radio show back in the States advertising Doublemint Gum. In January 1940 *Melody Ranch* began on the CBS network featuring Autry's theme song, "Back in the Saddle Again."

In the Pacific Coast League, the 1940s began with Lou "the Mad Russian" Novikoff winning the Triple Crown while playing for the Angels, then joining the Chicago Cubs, who purchased his contract for $100,000. Sacramento was led by player-manager Pepper Martin, a former star for the Cardinals Gashouse Gang.

The Nashville Vols finished third in the Southern League in 1939, and Bert Haas won the league batting title with a .365 average. Then, in 1940, the Vols fielded one of their best teams ever and won the pennant handily, going 101-47 for a .682 winning percentage and finishing nine and a half games ahead of the second-place team. Members of the winning team included pitchers Boots Poffenberger, who won twenty-six games that year, and Johnny Sain, who later became a star pitcher in the majors. The Southern League all-star game was held in Nashville on July 8. At the end of the season, the Vols won the Shaughnessy Playoff and then swept Houston, the Texas League champ, in the Dixie Series.

Also during the 1940 season, Vol Charlie Gilbert made it to the major leagues, playing his first game for the Brooklyn Dodgers against the Boston Braves on April 16. The twenty-year-old hit leadoff and played center field. In an interesting coincidence, young Gilbert's major league debut came almost twenty-six years to the day after his father, Vol manager Larry Gilbert, made his debut in the majors playing center field on April 14, 1914, for the Boston Braves against the Brooklyn Dodgers. Also, Casey Stengel, who played for Brooklyn that day, was the manager of the Braves when they played Charlie Gilbert's Dodgers. And Bill Klem umpired both games, over a quarter-century apart!

In 1940 the Brooklyn Dodgers, under manager Leo Durocher, finished second with a lineup that included Dolf Camilli, Pee Wee Reese, Cookie Lavagetto, Pete Reiser, Joe Medwick, and Dixie Walker, the regular center fielder. The National League winner that year was the Cincinnati Reds, which faced the Detroit Tigers, led by Rudy York, Charlie Gehringer, Hank Greenberg, Earl Averill, and a pitching staff headed by Bobo Newsom, Schoolboy Rowe, Hal Newhouser, Dizzy Trout, and Tommy Bridges. The Tigers won the 1940 World Series in seven games.

In 1938 Republic Pictures came to Nashville to scout out the Grand Ole Opry for a movie based on the show. The owner of Republic, Herbert Yates, was no stranger to country music. Republic was known for their "B Western" and singing cowboy movies (they were responsible for the initial success of Gene Autry and Roy Rogers), which had made country music a national music. Also, Yates was head of the American Record Company, whose roster included Gene Autry and other country performers. But it was not until the Opry went on the NBC network—and was carried by more than forty stations across the country, reaching all the way to the West Coast—that Republic actually set about developing a movie.

In May 1940 Roy Acuff and his group, along with Uncle Dave Macon and Judge George D. Hay, went to Hollywood to perform in the movie *The Grand Ole Opry,* which starred the comedy group the Weaver Brothers and Elviry. While there Acuff achieved a bit of a reputation by refusing to put on cowboy clothes and insisting his group perform in southern mountain garb.

In September the world premiere for the movie was held at the Paramount Theater in Nashville, and several distinguished guests were in attendance, including World War I hero Alvin York and Tennessee governor Prentice Cooper. Portions of the premier were broadcast over the NBC network. The release of the motion picture was yet another step toward national recognition for the Opry and for country music radio shows.

Also in 1940 Roy Acuff compiled his first songbook, *Roy Acuff's Folio of Original Songs Featured over WSM Grand Ole Opry,* which signaled his entry into the music publishing business. This would have a major impact on country music in the coming years.

The next year, 1941, is remembered in baseball history as the year Ted Williams hit .406 and Joe DiMaggio hit in fifty-six consecutive games. DiMaggio led the New York Yankees into the World Series against the Brooklyn Dodgers, and the Yankees took the Series four games to one. With the escalation of war in Europe, this turned out to be the last "normal" season for major league baseball until the 1946 season. In Nashville the Vols played seven consecutive doubleheaders between August 31 and September 7 but finished second in the league; however, they did win the Shaughnessy Playoff and the Dixie Series that year. That season Vol pitcher Boots Poffenberger, after winning twenty-six games in 1940, ended his career in the Southern Association when he pitched in a game drunk, lost his temper at an umpire's decision, and threw the ball at the ump. He never played in the Southern Association again. Fans from that time remember him as "looney" even on his best days. Such antics were not unknown to early country music performers either, and it was usually booze that caused the trouble.

In the summer of 1941 (probably mid-to-late July) Pee Wee King and the Golden West Cowboys, with singer Eddy Arnold, returned to Nashville and the Grand Ole Opry from WHAS in Louisville, where they had spent the previous year. Shortly after their return, fiddler Redd Stewart was drafted, and at about that time the Golden West Cowboys agreed to be part of the Camel Caravan, a troupe of performers who played at military bases all over the United States. There were a number of Camel Caravans, all organized by the William Esty advertising agency and sponsored by the R. J. Reynolds Tobacco Company (which manufactured Camel brand cigarettes). These Caravan visits to military bases all had a patriotic theme: military personnel in uniform got into the concerts for free, and many concerts were held on military bases. Also, during the show cigarette girls passed out free samples of Camel cigarettes to military personnel in the audience. King's group toured military bases nonstop from November 1941 until December 1942, helping make country music a "national" music by exposing it to so many servicemen.

On Saturday night, December 6, 1941, *The Grand Ole Opry* was broadcast live from the War Memorial Building. Featured on that night's show were Roy Acuff, Uncle Dave Macon, Minnie Pearl, Robert Lunn, Uncle Natchel, the Missouri Mountaineers, the Possum Hunters, the Williams Sisters, Tommy Thompson, Bill Monroe, Sam and Kirk McGee, Zeke Clements, the Gully Jumpers, the Fruit Jar Drinkers, and the Crook Brothers.

The next day, Sunday, December 7, Gene Autry was ready to begin his CBS radio show, *Melody Ranch,* when the announcer interrupted to report on the Japanese attack on Pearl Harbor. Autry and his crew went on with the show after the announcement. The Camel Caravan troupe from the Grand Ole Opry arrived in San Antonio, Texas, scheduled to perform at Kelly Field, Randolph Field, and Fort Sam Houston the next day.

Shortly after the United States entered the war, Gene Autry finished the movie he was making and enlisted in the Army Air Corps and served in the Asian theater. An avid baseball fan who tried to schedule personal tours so he would be in New York during World Series time and could catch a game or two if one of the New York teams played (a likely prospect during those years), Gene Autry's dream of seeing major league baseball in Los Angeles was crushed when Pearl Harbor was attacked. Earlier in the year Don Barnes, owner of the

St. Louis Browns, had decided to move the team to Los Angeles, and he and Phil Wrigley had agreed that Barnes would purchase the Angels and Wrigley Field for $1 million. The move to Los Angeles by the Browns was the first item on the agenda for the winter meetings of the American League, scheduled for Monday, December 8, 1941. But after the attack, the move was voted down at the meeting because the west coast was perceived to be dangerous. That event would make it possible for Autry to own the first American League team in Los Angeles twenty years later.

On Monday evening, December 8, 1941, President Franklin Roosevelt delivered the speech that told of "the date that will live in infamy" and announced that the United States would declare war on Japan. A few days later the United States declared war on Germany as well. And so the year 1941 ended with the United States in a world war, embarked on a mission that would forever change baseball, country music, the nation itself, and, indeed, the whole world.

5

The World War II Years

Eleven million Americans served in World War II, including 500 major league and 3,500 minor league ballplayers. Detroit slugger Hank Greenberg was among the first drafted, in 1941 before the United States had entered the war, and Bob Feller, the star Cleveland pitcher, enlisted in the navy right after Pearl Harbor. A number of country music artists were either drafted or enlisted, including singing cowboy Gene Autry, who joined the army in early 1942 and flew planes throughout the war.

Prior to the war, the success of the singing cowboys in Hollywood had created a demand for songwriters to write songs for the movies starring Autry, Tex Ritter, Roy Rogers, and others. One of the best of these songwriters was Fred Rose, who during the 1920s wrote pop hits such as "Deed I Do," "Red Hot Mama," and

"Honest and Truly." In 1933 Rose moved to Nashville and appeared on an afternoon show, *The Freddie Rose Song Shop* on WSM, and then to Hollywood in 1938 to write songs for Gene Autry's movies, penning "Be Honest with Me" and others. Rose moved back to Nashville in the summer of 1942 after Autry joined the armed services (because his wife preferred living there), and he soon had another afternoon show on WSM. He became acquainted with a number of Grand Ole Opry performers, including Roy Acuff, who approached him about starting a publishing company. Rose agreed, and the Acuff-Rose Publishing Company was incorporated in October 1942. This became a most successful music business and made Nashville a good place for songs and songwriters. In addition to his role as a publisher, signing and developing other songwriters, Rose played a major role in bringing the pop song format to country music as he had done for the singing cowboys in Hollywood. This would change country music significantly, as the songs used country themes in their lyrics while musically adapting the pop song format of verse, chorus, and bridge.[1]

In Nashville 1942 was a banner year for both baseball and country music. Out at the Sulphur Dell ballpark the Nashville Vols again finished second in the league and won the Shaughnessy Playoff and the Dixie Series against Shreveport. At the end of the year the Camel

Caravan Tour of Opry performers returned home after traveling more than 50,000 miles to perform in 175 shows in nineteen states for audiences at army camps, hospitals, air fields, and naval and marine bases.

World War II drastically changed domestic life in the United States as young men joined the armed forces and the home front mobilized for war on two fronts. Country music suffered from gas and tire rationing, which limited travel and touring, but was helped by its proximity to military bases. Because of the warm climate and availability of cheap land, the government built a number of bases in the South, and here about half the servicemen—or about six million young men—received basic training and were introduced to country music. In Nashville alone more than a million soldiers on weekend leave visited the city during 1942, and many of them saw *The Grand Ole Opry*. The Ralston Purina Company, another national sponsor, bought time on the show beginning in January 1943, which helped host Eddy Arnold become a national star.

The Opry continued with its shows throughout the war, and by October 1943 was broadcast on 125 stations over NBC's national network. Additionally, transcriptions of the Opry were sent out all over the country and put on Armed Forces Radio. In 1944 *Billboard* magazine began to feature a national chart of country music—which it called "folk"—giving the music even more attention. Also during the war pop singer Bing

Crosby recorded a number of country songs, which took the music to an even larger audience.

Major league baseball wasn't so lucky. It was hurt because so many key players served in the armed forces. In 1942 attendance at major league games fell to 8.8 million and to 7.7 million in 1943, and the Philadelphia Phillies went bankrupt in 1943. Still, major league baseball continued to be played, a result of President Franklin Roosevelt's letter on January 15, 1942, to Commissioner Kenesaw Landis giving the go-ahead for baseball to be played during the war, although healthy players would still be eligible for the draft. Because of the wage freeze and the fact that most of the high-salaried players were drafted into service, the operating expenses for club owners went down. And gas rationing forced people to stay close to home, which meant that a short train trip to a major league park was a good outing for entertainment.

During the 1942 season a number of major leaguers still weren't called up, so the season saw some pretty good baseball played. The St. Louis Cardinals, which featured Stan Musial (in his rookie season), Terry Moore, Enos Slaughter, shortstop Marty Marion, catcher Walker Cooper, and pitchers Mort Cooper and Johnny Beazley, won the National League pennant. They faced the Yankees in the World Series and beat the New York team in four straight games.

The Cardinals were the favorite major league team of many Nashville residents, because St. Louis was the closest city in major league baseball and because Nash-villians could pick up the signal from the St. Louis radio station that broadcast Cardinals games. Eddy Arnold had lived in St. Louis before moving to Nashville, and he continued to follow the Cardinals. And the Cardinals loved country music. A group of players led by Dizzy Dean called themselves the Mudcats and played and sang country songs like "Birmingham Jail" in the team's clubhouse. It was a good time for Cardinal fans; the St. Louis club won again in 1943 and again faced the Yankees in the World Series. But it was a different Series for both teams; the Cardinals had lost Enos Slaughter, Terry Moore, and Johnny Beazley to the armed services, and the Yankees were without Joe DiMaggio, Phil Rizzuto, Frank Crosetti, and Tommy Henrich. But the Cardinals still had Stan Musial and the Cooper brothers, Walker and Mort, and the Yankees still had Bill Dickey, Joe Gordon, and Charlie Keller. The Yankees won this World Series in five games.

By 1943 major league stars serving in the war included Ted Williams, Dom DiMaggio, Johnny Pesky, Pee Wee Reese, Pete Reiser, Johnny Mize, and Joe DiMaggio. In 1944 Joe Gordon, Charlie Keller, Mickey Vernon, Billy Herman, Arky Vaughan, and Kirby Higbe were also in the armed forces. At this point, with its dwindling ranks, the major leagues began recruiting players from Latin America, who were not eligible for the draft. Fifty Latin players played in the majors during the war years. Black American players, however, were still not allowed to play for any major league team.

During the war the majors was filled with players classified 4-F because of some chronic physical condition that excluded them from military service, including Lou Boudreau, Junior Stephens, and Hal Newhouser. There were also a number of aging ballplayers who received a few extra years in the majors because of the player shortage, among them Jimmie Foxx, Paul Waner, Babe Herman, and Luke Appling, who at the age of thirty-eight in 1943 won his second American League batting title. This is also the period when the majors, desperate for players, had fifteen-year-old Joe Nuxhall make his major league pitching debut and had one-armed outfielder Pete Gray playing for the St. Louis Browns.

Country music saw fewer of its stars leave the industry for service in the war. Eddy Arnold and Ernest Tubb did not serve, and Bob Wills served only briefly. And while a number of side musicians, as well as some executives, served during the war (including Jack Stapp of WSM), by and large country music stars continued to perform during the war, often using their talent to raise money for bond drives.

Minor league baseball was hit hard during these years. The Texas League stopped play in 1942, and by the end of the 1944 season only ten minor league circuits were still playing, including the Pacific Coast League, the American Association, International

League, and the Southern Association. On July 9, 1943, Nashville hosted the Southern Association all-star game. Nashville won the Southern Association pennant in 1943 and 1944 and featured some stellar performances by its players. In 1943 Vol Ed Sauer took the league batting title with a .368 mark, making it three years in a row and four years out of five that a Nashville Vol had been the Southern Association batting champ. During 1944 the Southern Association played a split season: during the first half of the season the Vols finished fifth, but in the second half the Vols edged Atlanta by one game to take the second-half title. In a playoff for the pennant against the Memphis Chicks, Nashville trailed three games to one before winning three straight to win the title on September 20, 1944.

The West Coast felt threatened throughout World War II; there was a constant fear that Japanese planes, ships, and submarines would attack their coast, a fear that led the government to place Japanese Americans in interment camps during the war. On March 24, 1942, Lieutenant General John DeWitt granted formal military permission for Pacific Coast League play, although beginning on August 20 night games were banned for the rest of that season and the next.

The Los Angeles Angels won the 1942 pennant. One of their stars was first baseman Eddie Waitkus (who was the inspiration for author Bernard Malmud's book *The Natural* when, in 1949 while playing for the Philadelphia Phillies, he was wounded by an infatuated girl). In

1943 the Angels dominated the league with right fielder Andy Pafko winning MVP honors. The Angels won the pennant again in 1944, and that season night games resumed. That was also the season when two Pacific League all-star games were held—one in Hollywood and the other in San Francisco, both on August 7.

Baseball was still played, but it was often former major leaguers and those not quite ready for professional baseball who filled out Pacific Coast League rosters. For the Hollywood Stars, player-manager Charlie Root, forty-four years old and a seventeen-year National League veteran, compiled a 15-5 pitching record in 1943, and another former major leaguer, Babe Herman, also played for the Stars.

Even though its ranks were not significantly reduced, the recording industry also had a tough time during the war. From August 1, 1942, until December 1, 1944, a strike called by the musician's union president James Caesar Petrillo brought the industry to a halt for most labels. In the fall of 1943 Decca capitulated to the union; however, RCA Victor and Columbia continued to hold out until they began to run out of stockpiled recordings and releases by a cappella groups proved commercially unsuccessful. Finally, RCA Victor and Columbia reached an agreement with the union and the strike ended.

Although there was a strike against recordings, the

armed forces were still able to make V-Discs, and these records were sent around the world to those serving in the military. There wasn't much country music recorded on V-Discs, which featured mostly American popular music by artists such as Bing Crosby, Glenn Miller, and Duke Ellington. American music received international exposure on a large scale for the first time. Armed Forces Radio, developed during World War II to boost troop morale, played a large part in introducing the world to American music.

Shortly after the recording ban was lifted, the first recording session for a major label in Nashville took place on December 4, 1944. This would mark the "official" beginning of Nashville as a major recording center, when Eddy Arnold recorded four songs for Victor.

By the start of the 1945 baseball season, about 60 percent of the men who had been on a major league team in 1941 were serving in the military, although few saw any combat action. In fact, a number of major leaguers played baseball during the war on teams representing bases such as the Norfolk Naval Training Station, the Great Lakes Naval Training Station, and the Bainbridge Naval Training Center. And like American music, which reached the world during the war through V-Discs, baseball was played around the globe by major league players who appeared in the Armed Forces World Series featuring navy and army teams. Also, it proved to be a great pickup game for American service-men with a ball, bat, and some time on their hands.

In 1945 the St. Louis Browns (still in St. Louis, and not in Los Angeles, because of the war), perennial los-ers in the American League, managed to win their only pennant. For years a money loser as well as a loser on the field, the Browns posted an 89-65 record in 1945, the worst of any pennant winner in the twentieth cen-tury. They faced their hometown rivals the Cardinals, who had won 105 games during the season. The Cardi-nals won the six-game Series after losing two of the first three.

Meanwhile, back at the Grand Ole Opry it was business as usual. Four years after the United States had officially entered the war, the Opry was still being broadcast over WSM featuring performers Pee Wee King, Wally Fowler, Minnie Pearl, Paul Howard, Er-nest Tubb, Lew Childre, Uncle Dave Macon, Eddy Ar-nold, Roy Acuff, the Duke of Paducah, Bill Monroe, Clyde Moody, and the Fruit Jar Drinkers. During the war the Opry had grown stronger—Minnie Pearl, Rod Brasfield, Ernest Tubb, and Eddy Arnold had all joined—and a one-hour Saturday matinee had been added. Also, in 1943 the Opry had moved to the Ryman Auditorium, which would be called "the Mother Church of Country Music" and which would be home to the Opry during its peak years after the war.

In California Roy Rogers had been promoted as "King of the Cowboys" by Republic Pictures while

Gene Autry was off in the Army Air Corps. By the end of 1945 Autry was back in Los Angeles. He thought his contract with Republic had run out during the time he was in the service, so he set out to start his own production company aligned with Columbia Pictures. Herbert Yates, head of Republic, thought otherwise, however, and insisted that Autry was still under contract. Finally it was resolved that Autry would star in some more Republic Pictures before starting his own production company. Autry also resumed his radio show, although at first it was limited to fifteen minutes instead of thirty minutes because the radio schedule was so crowded.

Radio was a major factor in the growth of both baseball and country music during this time. By the end of the war about 90 percent of American households had a radio and many of them listened to country music on Saturday nights and major league baseball games, especially the World Series.

6

After the War

The post–World War II years 1946–49 were golden ones for baseball and country music. The major league rosters were filled with returning players, and during the 1946 season only about 20 percent of the players from the previous year were in the lineups; instead, returning players filled the rosters. The paid attendance for regular season games that year was a record 18.5 million. Country music artists with the Grand Ole Opry were back on the road again, constantly traveling and often listening to Cardinals games on their car radios.

During the 1946 season Ted Williams hit .342 for Boston, and pitchers Tex Hughson and Dave "Boo" Ferriss and players Dom DiMaggio, Johnny Pesky, Bobby Doerr, and Rudy York all had outstanding seasons to lead the Red Sox, managed by Joe Cronin, to the American League title. In the National League the

Brooklyn Dodgers and St. Louis Cardinals were tied at the end of the season; in a three game playoff the Cardinals, led by Stan Musial (who hit .365 to lead the league), Enos Slaughter, Marty Marion, and Terry Martin, triumphed. In the World Series the Cardinals won in seven games, when, in the last game, "Country" Slaughter scored from first base on a single by Harry Walker when Boston shortstop Johnny Pesky hesitated in his relay throw. It was the third world championship for the St. Louis club in five years. Boston's Ted Williams, playing in his only World Series, faced the "Ted Williams shift" when he came to bat with no one on base. The "shift" saw all the Cardinal players shift to the right of second base except the left fielder. Williams ignored the defense, kept pulling the ball, and hit only five singles in seven games, hitting just .200 in his only World Series.

Although 1946 marked a return to regular major league play, there were some significant changes made in organized baseball. That year the players challenged team owners through a new organization, the American Baseball Guild. The contested reserve clause was kept, but players received "more meal money on road trips and $25 per week for spring-training expenses . . . a salary minimum of $5,000, a twenty-five-percent limit on cuts from one year to the next, an assured World Series pool of at least $250,000, and a pension plan . . . [that] guaranteed a pension to players with five years of big-league service" that would be funded from World Series and All-Star Game revenues.[1]

Baseball commissioner Kenesaw Mountain Landis, who had died in November 1944, had been replaced in March 1945 by Albert B. "Happy" Chandler, a U.S. senator from Kentucky. Shortly after taking office, Chandler, answering a question about allowing blacks to play in the majors, had stated, "If a black boy can make it on Okinawa and Guadalcanal, hell, he can make it in baseball."[2] During his tenure as commissioner, Landis had adamantly refused to consider allowing blacks into the major leagues. In August 1945 Brooklyn Dodgers general manager Branch Rickey met secretly with Jackie Robinson in Rickey's Ebbets Field office to discuss playing in the majors. On October 23, 1945, Robinson signed a contract to play the 1946 season with the Montreal Royals, the International League farm club for the Dodgers. The following January the major league representatives voted 15 to 1 against adding black players to their rosters (Branch Rickey was the lone dissenter), but Chandler privately assured Rickey that the commissioner's office would not stand in the way of Rickey's plan to add black players to Brooklyn's roster. Leading the opposition against integration was Larry MacPhail of the New York Yankees, Tom Yawkey of the Red Sox, Sam Breadon of the Cardinals, and Phil Wrigley of the Cubs.

On April 15, 1947, Jackie Robinson played first base for the Brooklyn Dodgers against the Boston Braves. Red Barber, the announcer for the Dodgers games, described 1947 as "the year all hell broke loose." In July the American League saw its first black player when Cleveland owner Bill Veeck signed Larry Doby. With the signing of these players, black fans started abandoning the Negro leagues and rooted for major league teams. Both Doby and Robinson faced jeers and taunts from fans and fellow players alike all that year, but at the end of the year Robinson managed to win Rookie of the Year honors as he led the Dodgers to the National League pennant.

The 1947 World Series featured a subway series between the New York Yankees and Brooklyn Dodgers. In the fourth game at Ebbets Field, Yankee pitcher Bill Bevens had a no-hitter with two outs in the ninth (although he had walked ten and the score was 2–1) when he gave up his only hit—a double off the right field wall to pinch-hitter Cookie Lavagetto that drove in two runs and gave the Dodgers a 3–2 victory. But the Yankees, with stars Joe DiMaggio, Phil Rizzuto, Tommy Henrich, Yogi Berra, Allie Reynolds, Joe Page, and Spud Chandler, rebounded to win the World Series.

In 1948 20.8 million paying fans watched major league regular season games. That same year baseball's greatest hero, Babe Ruth, died in August at the age of fifty-three after a two-year battle with throat cancer. The American League season ended with a tie between the Cleveland Indians and Boston Red Sox; the Indians won the one-game playoff game 8–3 and then faced the Boston

Braves in the World Series. The Cleveland club won the World Series, with 86,200 fans in the stands for game five—the biggest crowd for a major league game.

Baseball as a business was booming, and the promotional activities of Bill Veeck with the Cleveland Indians set the pace, although his "fireworks, giveaways, swimsuit pageants, clown acts, and an assortment of other 'bonus attractions'" brought complaints that he was "cheapening the National Pastime." Veeck replied, "A baseball team is a commercial venture, operating for a profit. The idea that you don't have to . . . hustle your product the way General Motors hustles its products is baseball's most pernicious enemy."[3] However, for most baseball owners there seemed to be no need to "hustle" to gain fans; there was always a line waiting to buy tickets before each game.

In 1949 paid attendance for major league games fell by about 600,000, although that seemed little cause for alarm after the record 1948 season attendance. In the 1949 World Series the New York Yankees, under new manager Casey Stengel, defeated the Brooklyn Dodgers in another subway series. This 1949 season marked the beginning of the Yankee "dynasty" that saw them win thirteen more American League pennants and eight more World Series championships over the next fifteen years. This was great for Yankee fans, but according to historian Charles Alexander, the Yankee dynasty would be "one of the principal ills besetting baseball in the 1950s."[4]

In 1949 the minor leagues were also doing extremely well. There were fifty-nine minor league teams, from Class AAA to Class D, and total paid admissions reached 42 million tickets sold. For most baseball fans in America, minor league baseball was what they followed most closely. Outside the ten cities with major leagues teams—New York had three; Chicago, Boston, Philadelphia, and St. Louis each had two; Cleveland, Detroit, Washington, Cincinnati, and Pittsburgh each had one—fans across the country attended minor league games in record numbers.

The period 1939 to 1949 was the peak of baseball in Nashville as the Southern Association Vols drew outstanding attendance. The Vols won their last pennant in 1949; that year they had 228,034 fans come to the Sulphur Dell. In 1925 the Sulphur Dell attracted a paid attendance of 178,633 for the season; that figure was not topped until 1946 when the postwar boom saw 213,284 fans come to the Vol games. During the 1947 season Vols catcher Rube Walker hit safely in ten straight at-bats, and Ted Kluszewski of the Memphis Chicks won the league batting title with a .377 mark. In 1948 Nashville Vol Smoky Burgess won the Southern Association batting title with a .386 mark. Each year saw increased attendance, with the top year of 1948 reaching 269,893. In 1949 attendance dropped to 228,034; this was blamed on a rainy spring but also marked the beginning of the decline of minor league baseball in Nashville.

At the end of the 1948 season Larry Gilbert stepped down as manager of the Nashville Vols after managing in the Southern Association for twenty-five years. In his last season Gilbert had again led the Vols to the Southern Association pennant, and on September 8, 1948, he was feted at the ballpark for his outstanding career. The next year, with new manager Rollie Hemsley, a former major leaguer who had spent nineteen years as a catcher (1928–44, 1946–47) with the Pittsburgh Pirates, Chicago Cubs, Cincinnati Reds, St. Louis Browns, Cleveland Indians, New York Yankees, and Philadelphia Phillies, Nashville took the Southern Association pennant. The key period was from August 10 on when the Vols won twenty-five of thirty-one games. Vols fans in 1949 would remember Carl "Swish" Sawatski, who was the MVP for the Southern Association that year, and Babe Barna, a thirty-four-year-old Hungarian who hit .341 with forty-two home runs and 138 runs batted in. On April 19, playing only six innings, Barna hit three home runs and two singles and drove in nine runs. The forty-two-year-old Hemsley also played in 1949, hitting .317 in fifty-six games at six positions. He suffered a fractured left thumb that year while coaching at third (and trying to stop a foul grounder); the next year he would be signed to manage Columbia, a St. Louis Cardinal farm club in the American Association.

The Sulphur Dell was still popular with fans and unpopular with players, who sometimes hit a line drive off the right field fence and then got thrown out at first.

The right field fence was short, and the right fielder played in a "hole" as the ground made a steep climb to the fence. First basemen often played balls hit off the grandstand in right while right fielders had to run up-hill to make a catch at the fence.

On the West Coast the Pacific Coast League attempted to become the third major league during baseball's winter meetings in December 1945. The league petitioned the American and National Leagues to be free from the major league draft and be able to option Coast League players to other teams in AAA baseball without losing "ownership." The request was denied by the majors, but they did promise to reconsider the proposal at some time in the future. Meanwhile, the independent teams in the Coast League (the Los Angeles Angels, owned by the Chicago Cubs, was the only team owned by a major league franchise) worked on a five-year plan to expand their stadiums to meet major league standards. Sacramento and Portland had markets that might be too small for major league franchises, so the idea of adding Denver, Houston, and Dallas to the league was considered. Leading this movement to join the majors after the 1950 season was Paul I. Fagan, owner of the San Francisco Seals. Fagan was a wealthy businessman who made Seals Stadium a first-rate facility and paid manager Lefty O'Doul and his star players top dollar (more than they could earn in the majors). However, other club owners did not have

Fagan's wealth, and so the idea of this third major league could never be realized.[5]

The Oakland Oaks of the Pacific Coast League was managed by Casey Stengel. In 1947 the Oaks featured twenty-year-old rookie Billy Martin and "Nine Old Men," former major leaguers, including Ernie Lombardi, Cookie Lavagetto, and Nick Etten. In 1946 the Pacific Coast League had 3,718,716 paid admissions and in 1947 4,068,432. In 1947 the combined attendance for the Los Angeles and Hollywood teams was over 1,100,000. In 1948 there was a slight decline in attendance—the league sold 400,000 fewer seats, with Los Angeles and Hollywood combined attracting just under a million fans. (L.A. had 576,373 and Hollywood had 416,725.)

Late in the 1947 season the Hollywood Stars and Los Angeles Angels began televising their home games; during the 1948 and 1949 season they increased their TV exposure at the expense of paid attendance. However, in 1949 the league's attendance figures increased by 90,000. Just prior to that season Hollywood had switched its major league affiliation from the Chicago White Sox to the Brooklyn Dodgers. Because the Dodgers had many top players, they needed another AAA club for these prospects to get playing time. The Hollywood Stars, under manager Fred Haney, won the Pacific Coast League pennant in 1949, and league MVP was Stars centerfielder Irv Noren.

Just as television was starting to change baseball in Los Angeles, it was also beginning to affect the singing cowboys. Gene Autry and Roy Rogers still starred in movies and had popular network radio shows, but they were already eyeing television as a future outlet for their talents.

In 1946 there were eight million records sold in America, and country music accounted for 13.2 percent of sales—topped only by "popular" with 50 percent and classical with 18.9 percent. The 550,000 jukeboxes, which before the war accounted for most of the sales of country records, now accounted for only about 10 percent of the total. Part of the reason for increased country record sales to consumers was the exposure country music was receiving on local shows and network shows thanks to the disc jockeys playing records on the radio.

World War II had brought Americans together around the radio to hear news of the world. People were employed because of the defense-based economy and were making money they could not spend because of the rationing of goods, the limited availability of consumer items, and the encouragement of savings by the government through their war bond drives. So after the war ended, a huge number of radio sets were sold. By the end of 1947, 93 percent of American households owned a radio. But 1947 was also the beginning of the television revolution; just when radio was at the height of its popularity, TV made took its first steps toward replacing radio as the dominant medium in the United States.

The number of radio stations exploded after World War II. In 1946 there were five hundred new stations licensed by the FCC; in 1948 there were an additional four hundred. Disk jockeys became increasingly important because there was not enough "live" talent to go around; also, playing records was easier and cheaper than hiring live talent. And records offered a wide variety of music—including country and rhythm and blues—that consumers wanted but could not get on network radio. So small stations playing records by disk jockeys proliferated. This trend ran parallel with the increased number of new small, independent record labels forming and recording country and rhythm and blues music. The major labels were locked into the pop sound that evolved from the Big Band era, with vocalists replacing the bandleaders as the "stars" but still featuring a smooth, sentimental pop sound.

There were changes at the radio network level for country music after the war. In 1946 NBC cancelled *National Barn Dance* on WLS in Chicago after star Red Foley left to join WSM and the Grand Ole Opry. Foley was replaced by Rex Allen, who left for Hollywood in 1949. At this time the WLS *National Barn Dance* moved to the ABC radio network but was cancelled there after about a year. By 1945 *Boone County Jamboree* in Cincinnati had been renamed *Midwestern Hayride,* and in 1948 it began to be featured on TV. *Dixie Jamboree* on WBT in Charlotte appeared on the regional CBS radio network during World War II; it evolved into *Carolina Hayride* and from 1946 was broadcast over CBS on Saturday nights. *Louisiana Hayride* was formed in 1948 on KWKH in Shreveport, Louisiana; this show and others appeared on CBS as *Saturday Night, Country Style* on a rotating basis.

In terms of technology, 1948 saw a great leap forward. ABC radio went all-tape, using the German-developed Magnetophone technology, the forerunner to analog tape that revolutionized the recording industry. Prior to this, recordings were done directly to disc. Also, in June 1948 Columbia Records premiered the 33 ⅓ rpm record, and in December RCA brought out the 45 rpm. These two new technologies on vinyl would eventually replace the old 78s.

But 1948 also saw some setbacks in the music industry. There was virtually no music recorded in 1948 because of a strike called by James Caesar Petrillo, head of the American Federation of Musicians, that lasted from January until December 1948. By the end of that period, most of the Big Bands had disbanded, effectively ending the Big Band era, though a few would regroup after 1948, and some even survived into the 1960s. The 1948 strike was Petrillo's last hurrah. He had become unpopular for calling a strike during World War II, even after President Roosevelt had requested that he not do so. Further, some alleged he was a member of the mafia, and Congress had accused him of being a racketeer. Finally, the Taft-Hartley Act, passed over President Harry Truman's veto in June 1948, limited the power of unions.

In country music the years 1946 to 1949 marked the time when two "centers" emerged: Nashville and Los Angeles. In Nashville *The Grand Ole Opry* became the top country music show, a result of its competition losing ground as well as the Opry's commitment to signing top name talent. In recordings Nashville-based Eddy Arnold sold more records than anybody else in country music; in fact, Arnold, with hits such as "Bouquet of Roses" and "I'll Hold You in My Heart," sold more records than most pop music acts. By the end of the 1940s other Opry-based stars, such as Ernest Tubb, Hank Williams, Bill Monroe, Roy Acuff, Little Jimmie Dickens, and Red Foley, were also major sellers. A recording studio was established in Nashville at the Tulane Hotel, a block from the WSM offices, by three WSM engineers. The studio was busy recording local advertisements as well as national recording artists, beginning with Ernest Tubb and Red Foley. In September 1946 Hank Williams came to Nashville and signed a songwriting contract with Fred Rose and the

Acuff-Rose Publishing Company. In late 1946 Williams began his recording career, and in 1949 he joined the Grand Ole Opry.

By that time *The Grand Ole Opry* had become a major profit center for WSM radio. An article in *Variety* in October 1949 noted that WSM grossed about $600,000 that year, with around $400,000 of that coming from the Opry. In addition to income from radio advertising, the Opry owned an agency that booked its acts. This booking agency grossed $640,000, collecting 15 percent of the income its artists made on personal appearances while the Opry itself earned $275,000 from the paid attendance at its Saturday-night shows. That year the Opry also made an agreement with the War Department for some of its artists to do a tour of military bases in Europe.[6]

In addition to national exposure of the Opry's network show on NBC, country music gained attention through articles in national periodicals and appearances at Carnegie Hall (headlined by Ernest Tubb) and Constitution Hall in Washington (headlined by Eddy Arnold). Artists such as Eddy Arnold and Ernest Tubb had their own network radio shows, and the demand for personal appearances kept country artists constantly on the road.

In Los Angeles the creation of a major label, Capitol, meant country artists on the West Coast, such as Tex Ritter, Merle Travis, Tennessee Ernie Ford, Spade Cooley, and Wesley Tuttle, would be recorded. The singing cowboys were still going strong; Gene Autry, Roy Rogers and Tex Ritter were all regularly releasing movies with songs. The Los Angeles area also had strong country music radio programs, from Gene Autry's and Roy Roger's network programs to *Hometown Jamboree,* hosted by Cliffie Stone. A top club, the Riverside Rancho, featured live country entertainment. Even though by the end of the 1940s there was probably more country music recorded in California than in Nashville, the country music industry would be overshadowed by the movie and, later, pop music, industries. And increasingly Nashville got credit for being the "center" of the country music business. By the end of the 1940s this business had gotten pretty big; it accounted for about a fourth of the profits from the major recording labels.

7

The Fifties

Paid attendance continued to decline for major league baseball games in 1950. Only 17,227,000 fans paid to see major league games in 1950, and in 1952 only 15 million showed up, which meant a drop in paid attendance of roughly 25 percent since 1948. The minor leagues suffered even more; the 42 million who paid to see minor league baseball in 1949 plummeted to 15.5 million by 1956, and the fifty-nine minor leagues in 1949 dropped to thirty-three in 1953 and then to twenty-eight in 1957. The tradition of minor league baseball in small cities and large towns had mostly vanished by 1960.

There were a variety of reasons for this decline. First, housing patterns in the post–World War II boom found people moving from cities and towns to the suburbs. This was encouraged by the federal government, which made loans available to veterans if they would buy a *new* house, which meant a home in the suburbs. Furthermore, the government encouraged car travel by lowering taxes on gasoline and through the construction of roads at the expense of public transportation. Also, in 1932 General Motors had formed a consortium, National City Lines, that included Firestone, Standard Oil, and Mack Truck to purchase city trolley transportation systems and tear up the tracks in order to sell more vehicles, tires, and gas. By 1956 this cabal had purchased the last of the electric rail lines and converted electric transit to mass transit buses.[1]

With the shift to the suburbs, people "developed distinctly suburban lifestyles, largely independent of what was happening in the city—at least as far as entertainment and recreation were concerned."[2] Compounding this problem was that major league baseball parks, built in the inner city, were in areas that were now in decay and becoming crime ridden as people fled the cities for the suburbs. This was especially a problem at night, when most baseball games were played. Families had to drive long distances to get to the ballpark and then had to find parking near the park, which was built at a time when public transportation was how fans got to ball games. Admission prices climbed even though the ballparks steadily deteriorated. The parks were built when steel girders were used for support, so fans often had to sit behind one of these girders, which hampered their view. And the seats were narrow and close together. During the game fans wondered if their cars were safe; after the games they wondered if they would be safe while they walked to their cars. Then, once in their cars, they faced a long drive back home. With most ball games starting at around 7:30 P.M. and lasting longer (games went from two hours to three hours and more) and the long drives into and back out of the city, fans were often not able to get back home before midnight. No wonder "millions of people simply decided it wasn't worth the trouble and turned to other things—backyard barbecues and bridge clubs; drive-in movies and neighborhood swimming parties; tennis, golf, and softball for themselves and Little League baseball for their children."[3] But while the 1950s saw dropped attendance at major and minor league games, it did not mean they watched fewer baseball games. With the rise of Little League in the suburbs, families often spent several evenings a week at a neighborhood ballpark watching young boys play baseball.

Little League baseball was started in 1938 by Carl Stotz in Williamsport, Pennsylvania. Stotz, twenty-eight and unemployed, enjoyed playing catch with his two nephews in the yard. (Stotz had a daughter but no sons.) As the boys, ages six and eight, played catch they kept up a running commentary of an imaginary game. And out of this Stotz developed the idea of boys playing a scaled-down version of a major league game. Stotz experimented with distances between the bases and from the mound to the plate and built a diamond on an unused field. He asked fifty-six companies for money to sponsor a team before one finally did. Stotz managed to get the community's interest, spoke at local meetings, and in 1939 took the boys to the New York World's Fair in their baseball uniforms. Then came World War II, and the volunteer coaches and umpires went off to fight; but when they returned, Little League took off. A Little League World Series was established, and U.S. Rubber was the principal backer. In 1951 the company incorporated the league, and Stotz was replaced as president. Stotz grew uncomfortable with the increased competitiveness of Little League play as the idea caught on; he wanted every boy to play, and safety was a major concern. Still, the idea took root and grew rapidly; by the mid-1950s there were large numbers of boys playing baseball and volunteer coaches all across the country in local suburban neighborhoods.

In 1950 the Philadelphia Phillies "Whiz Kids," led by Robin Roberts, Curt Simmons, Del Ennis, Richie Ashburn, and Jim Konstanty (who became the first relief pitcher to win the MVP award in the National League that year) won the National League pennant on the last day of the season when Dick Sisler's home run defeated the Brooklyn Dodgers. They faced the Yankees in the World Series, and the New York club, led by Phil Rizzuto (who won American League MVP honors that year), Joe DiMaggio, Whitey Ford, Vic Raschi, Allie Reynolds, Eddie Lopat, and Tommy Byrne, swept the Phillies.

After the 1950 season Branch Rickey lost a power struggle to Walter O'Malley, who became controlling owner of the Dodgers. Rickey moved to the Pittsburgh Pirates and began building that club's farm system. He also began making "bonus babies" of high school prospects, handing large amounts of money to young players to sign.

In 1951 the National League season ended with a tie between the Brooklyn Dodgers and the New York Giants. In the third game of the three-game playoff— with each team having won one game—the Giants were behind 4–2 with two men on base and two out in the bottom of the ninth. Dodger manager Charlie Dressen brought in Ralph Branca to relieve Don Newcombe with Bobby Thomson at bat. Thomson hit Branca's pitch into the left field stands at the Polo Grounds as announcer Ralph Hodges shouted, "The Giants win the pennant! The Giants win the pennant!" This "shot heard 'round the world" is perhaps one of the most dramatic moments in baseball history.

In the 1951 World Series the Yankees beat the Giants in five games. In 1952 it would be the Brooklyn Dodgers against the Yankees, with the Yanks winning again. If you were a baseball fan in New York it was heaven: either the Giants or Dodgers faced the Yankees in the World Series. But the rest of the country soon lost interest in rooting for teams that never made it to the Series. Sportswriters in New York championed the period as a "golden era" with heroes such as Mickey Mantle, Willie Mays, and Duke Snider vying for the title as best center fielder with New York fans, but it was increasingly difficult for baseball fans outside New York to remain enthusiastic about their teams.

Meanwhile, in Nashville in 1950–52 the country music industry was steadily finding its center, led by *The Grand Ole Opry* and the songs from Acuff-Rose Publishing. The biggest hit in 1950 was "Tennessee Waltz" by Patti Page, a song published by Acuff-Rose that, more than any other song up to this period, showed the popular music world that Nashville was a good source for songs. This led directly to pop artists such as Rosemary Clooney and Tony Bennett recording songs by Hank Williams, which were also published by Acuff-Rose.

In 1952 the Grand Ole Opry hosted a "Grand Ole Opry Birthday Celebration" and invited about one hundred country music disc jockeys from across the country to attend. By the next year the Country and Western Disc Jockey Association was formed, and the group's annual convention became the major national gathering for those involved in country music, further solidifying Nashville's claim as the capital of country music. The title "Music City U.S.A." was increasingly used to describe Nashville, a result of WSM announcer David Cobb's radio ad lib.

The link between country music and baseball grew stronger as major league players increasingly came from the South, where they had grown up on country music. And one former minor league player became a major country recording artist. Jim Reeves had gone to the University of Texas in 1942 on a baseball scholarship but dropped out to work in the shipyards of Houston and then play minor league ball in the St. Louis Cardinals organization. An injury ended his career in the late 1940s, and he began recording country music, cutting his first records in 1949. In April 1953 his first big hit, "Mexican Joe," reached number one. After a successful stint on *Louisiana Hayride* in Shreveport, Louisiana, he moved to Nashville.

January 1953 marked the inauguration of a new U.S. president, Dwight D. Eisenhower, a hero of World War II. This ended the Roosevelt era, which began in 1933 when Franklin Delano Roosevelt was first elected and ended with the second term of Harry Truman, Roosevelt's vice president who became president in April 1945 after FDR's death. In that summer of 1953 the Korean War ended. The past two decades had seen great changes and major upheavals—the Great Depression, World War II, the atomic bomb, the Korean War, and the numerous government programs that changed the role of government in American life—and America was now ready for the calm, "grandfatherly" image of Eisenhower.

Although the fifties have often been portrayed as a dull, uninteresting time, in reality the changes in the 1950s were as important as those made in the 1960s, which became known as an era of major change. This was particularly true in baseball and country music. In 1953 the Boston Braves moved to Milwaukee, and then in 1954 the St. Louis Browns moved and became the Baltimore Orioles. In 1958 the Brooklyn Dodgers and New York Giants moved west to Los Angeles and San Francisco, respectively. This furthered the decline of minor league baseball as the new cities—Milwaukee, Baltimore, Los Angeles, and San Francisco—had previously fielded strong minor league teams with large followings.

For country music the year 1953 began with the death of Hank Williams, who died en route from Alabama to Canton, Ohio, for a concert appearance. That same year Eddy Arnold, the most commercially successful artists in country music, split from his manager, Colonel Tom Parker. At the end of 1954 Fred Rose, one of the pioneers of the Nashville music business, the producer and publisher of Hank Williams, and the founder of Acuff-Rose Publishing, died, marking the end of an era in the country music business in Nashville.

The end of the singing cowboy also came in the early 1950s. Gene Autry made his last movies in 1953, and Roy Rogers had finished his "singing cowboy" movies the year before. Republic Pictures, the Hollywood studio that produced most of the singing cowboy movies, made its last singing cowboy movie in 1954 with Rex Allen. By this time, Autry and Rogers had begun to concentrate on television.

8

Baseball and Country Music on TV

Paid attendance at major and minor league baseball began declining in 1949 and throughout the 1950s baseball suffered the ongoing problem of attracting fans to games; at the same time baseball reached a national audience. The culprit and the hero for baseball's problems during this period was television.

Television was invented in 1925, and by 1928 the first home sets were being built. Television made its debut with the American public at the 1939 World's Fair in New York, and the first televised baseball game took place during the Fair, on May 17, 1939, when NBC broadcast in the New York area a college game between Princeton and Columbia. However, the Great Depression and then World War II hampered the development of the TV industry. In 1941 the Federal

Communications Commission authorized the broadcast of commercial television. On April 13, 1946, the DuMont Television Network went on the air. However, that year only 6,476 sets were produced. In 1947 there were 178,571 sets produced, mostly with ten-inch screens. They cost between $225 and $2,500, plus a five dollar antenna installation fee.

In 1947, the first year of TV programming, there were four networks: ABC, CBS, NBC, and DuMont. The first significant baseball telecast occurred in October 1947 when NBC broadcast the World Series over a four station "network." Since it was a subway series—the Yankees beat the Dodgers in seven games—it was easy to broadcast this game to the New York market in this early era of TV. It was an exciting Series; after the first two games were won by the Yankees, the Dodgers won the third. Then, in the fourth game, with the Yankees leading with two outs in the bottom of the ninth, Yankee pitcher Bill Bevans lost his no-hitter when pinch-hitter Cookie Lavagetto doubled in two runs to tie the Series. The Yankees won the fifth game and might have ended the Series in the sixth game except Al Gionfriddo robbed Joe DiMaggio of a home run with a great catch. The Yankees won the seventh and deciding game 5–2 behind the relief pitching of Joe Page. This game reached a television audience of about half a million people in the Northeast.

In 1948 television had its first full season of programming. During the first six months of the year there were 350,000 sets in American homes. Milton Berle became the first TV star with his *Texaco Star Theater*. Baseball broadcasts followed the pattern of radio broadcasts: the commissioner negotiated network coverage of the World Series and all-star games, with all the clubs sharing in the revenue, while individual clubs negotiated broadcast rights in their own markets. Broadcast revenue gave an added revenue stream to major league clubs but did not benefit all clubs equally. It undercut the appeal of minor league baseball because when people could see major league games in their own homes they were less likely to go out to a minor league ballpark. Television broadcasts also led to an imbalance within major league baseball. Clubs in New York and Chicago received substantial income from television, but the teams in smaller markets—like Washington, St. Louis, Cleveland and Cincinnati—did not receive nearly as much. For example, by 1959 the Yankees were receiving $1 million each season from TV broadcasts, while Washington was receiving only $150,000; this revenue gave the Yankees additional funds for building their team, which, in turn, helped perpetuate the team's dominance.

Baseball had a national audience for the televised World Series. The National Broadcasting Company (NBC) paid major league baseball $6 million for TV-radio rights to broadcast the 1951–56 Series and then paid $15 million for the 1957–62 broadcast rights. Interestingly, however, the first *regular* prime-time coverage of baseball occurred in the 1951 and 1952 baseball seasons when ABC broadcast women's baseball games. The National Women's Professional Baseball League games were popularly known as "Girls' Baseball" and followed the home games of one of the teams—the Queens of America.

Television's presence increased dramatically during the 1948–53 period; whereas in 1948 only 1 percent of American homes had TVs, 50 percent had sets by the end of 1953. In June 1953 the American Broadcasting Company (ABC) began broadcasting the "Game of the Week" to a national audience. Baseball had a national audience on radio for a number of years, with the Mutual Broadcasting System airing a daily radio game for years, but with the advent of ABC's "Game of the Week" millions of American baseball fans would finally see their first major league baseball games.

In 1955 the Columbia Broadcasting System (CBS) took over the "Game of the Week" and brought in Dizzy Dean to do the play-by-play for the Saturday (and sometimes Sunday) games. Dean, a southerner, was known for his fractured English ("Dean-isms" such as "slud into third" are still known) as well as for belting out Roy Acuff's hit "Wabash Cannonball" over the air. In fact, Dean cut a record of the song, and probably as many people heard Dean's version of the "Wabash Cannonball" as heard Acuff's country classic. They also heard Dean give Acuff the title "the King of Country

Music," which was worn proudly by Acuff for the rest of his life.

Like baseball, country music appeared on television through local shows in major cities with some occasional network exposure. There were four shows that featured country music on the networks during prime time in 1948. The first to appear was *Village Barn,* which debuted on May 17, 1948, and ran until May 29, 1950, on the NBC network. *Hayloft Hoedown* appeared on the ABC network on Saturday nights beginning on July 10 and ending on September 18. On September 29 *Kobb's Korner* appeared on the CBS network on Wednesday evenings, and it ran until June 15, 1949. *Saturday Night Jamboree* debuted on December 4 and ran until July 2, 1949, appearing on Saturday nights on the NBC network. All of these early programs were presented in a variety-show format.

The following year, 1949, was a little better, with the introduction of *ABC Barn Dance,* which was actually Chicago's *National Barn Dance* now broadcast on television. It was a half-hour show on Monday nights; it began in February 1949 and lasted until November. In 1950 there were three country music shows on prime-time TV: *Country Style,* which featured a lot of square dancing, and *Rhythm Rodeo* and *Windy City Jamboree,* both broadcast from Chicago.

At this point country music on TV still had a long way to go. The "country" shows that originated from

Chicago or New York—where the TV studios were—
were yokel-type shows that featured rube comedy. But
in 1951 the first significant country music shows began
to appear on TV, and these would become the forerunner for "real" country music on television.

Midwestern Hayride began on June 16, 1951, on the
NBC network and lasted until September 6, 1959. At
first it was broadcast on Saturday night, then on Tues-
days; in July 1957 it switched networks, moving over to
ABC, where it was broadcast on either Saturday or Sunday evenings. The show came out of either Dayton or
Cincinnati, Ohio, and proved to be a summer standby.

The first country music show hosted by a country
music star was *The Eddy Arnold Show,* which premiered
on July 14, 1952, on the CBS network. The show ran for
fifteen minutes on Mondays, Wednesdays, and Fridays;
it then moved over to NBC, where it appeared on
Tuesday and Thursdays. In April 1956 it became a half-
hour show on ABC, where it stayed until it ended on
September 28, 1956.

During the run of Eddy Arnold's show, several
other country music shows appeared on TV. *The Old
American Barn Dance* went on the air in the summer of
1953; this show, emceed by Bill Bailey, featured artists
such as Pee Wee King and Tennessee Ernie Ford. On
October 15, 1955, the Grand Ole Opry began broadcasting its shows regularly on the ABC network, with
regulars Carl Smith, Ernest and Justin Tubb, Hank
Snow, Minnie Pearl, Chet Atkins, Goldie Hill, Marty

Robbins, Rod Brasfield, Cousin Jody, Roy Acuff, June Carter, Jimmy Dickens, and the Louvin Brothers. This monthly show lasted about a year, with its final show airing on September 15, 1956.

The most important early country music show on TV was *The Ozark Jubilee,* which was broadcast on the ABC network on Saturday nights from Springfield, Missouri, beginning on January 22, 1955. Hosted by Red Foley, the show featured top country talent such as Webb Pierce, Jean Shepard, Hawkshaw Hawkins, Porter Wagoner, the Oklahoma Wranglers, Bobby Lord, Marvin Rainwater, Wanda Jackson, Billy Walker, Norma Jean, Leroy Van Dyke, Smiley Burnette, and Lew Childre. The theme song for the show was "Sugarfoot Rag," written and played by guitarist Hank Garland. The show became *The Country Music Jubilee* in July 1957 and then *Jubilee U.S.A.* beginning in August 1958. It ran until September 24, 1960, when it was abruptly cancelled by ABC, even though it was still extremely popular. The reason ABC gave for canceling the show was because it had the rights to the Gillette fights and wanted to carry them; however, the real reason was that Red Foley had been indicted for tax fraud and was preparing to stand trial as the 1960 season began. (Foley's first trial ended in a hung jury; his second in 1961 resulted in an acquittal.)

The major competitor for the Springfield show was the syndicated *Stars of the Grand Ole Opry,* which was produced by early 1955. In June 1955 NBC ran an Opry special, and ABC began its Opry broadcast in October 1955. But the Opry did not concentrate on TV the way the Springfield group did, preferring to stick with radio and its live shows.

The next major country music show to appear on television was *The Ford Show, Featuring Tennessee Ernie Ford,* more commonly called *The Tennessee Ernie Ford Show,* sponsored by Ford Motors. This show debuted on October 4, 1956, and ran until June 29, 1961; it aired on Thursday nights on the NBC network.

Although there was some country music on national network TV in the 1950s, the genre experienced its greatest success in local and syndicated programs. This parallels the story of country music on radio: a handful of country shows appeared on the network, yet numerous cities, mainly in the Southeast, broadcast country music programs as "barn dances" and early-morning and midday programs as well.

The Southeast tended to lag behind the rest of the country in getting TV sets; in the mid-1950s about 75 percent of the households in the Northeast and Midwest had TV sets, while only about 50 percent of southern households had sets. Also, people in cities were more likely to own a TV set—ownership ranged from 50 to 80 percent—while in rural households ownership ranged from 42 to 61 percent.

While television helped both baseball and country music by providing large, accessible audiences, it also hurt these entertainment industries by undermining their appeal to a live audience. For baseball this meant fewer fans paid to see games; for country music it meant being saddled with an image of yokels and rubes that the industry would work hard for years to overcome. Both baseball and country music had reached middle America. But while baseball became a sport loved by the middle class, country music was generally shunned by the middle class, which viewed the genre as backward, uncouth, and low class.

9

Radio in the Fifties

Country music continued to be heard on radio barn dances until the mid-1950s. In 1952 there were 176 stations carrying *The Prince Albert Show* from the Grand Ole Opry over the NBC radio network each Saturday night. In July 1954 *The Ozark Jubilee* began on KWTO in Springfield, Missouri; it was broadcast over the ABC radio network and then became a TV show on ABC.

There were also barn dances or country jamborees aired throughout the country. *Big D Jamboree* was on KRLD in Dallas and *Saturday Night Shindig* was on WFAA, also in Dallas; Houston had *Hometown Jamboree* on KNUX, and *Hollywood Barn Dance* came from Los Angeles on KNX. *Hometown Jamboree,* which Cliffie Stone began on KXLA in Los Angles in about 1949, and *Hayloft Jamboree* from WCOP in Boston also flourished in the 1950s. One of the most popular country music shows was the *Town Hall Party* from Los Angeles, which was carried by the NBC network. Other barn dances included *Hayloft Hoedown* from WFIL in Philadelphia; *Hoosier Hop* from WOWO in Fort Wayne, Indiana; *Roundup of Stars* in Tampa over WDAE; and *Old Dominion Barn Dance* on WRVA in Richmond, Virginia. Other cities with regular radio barn dances included Cleveland, Indianapolis, Yankton, South Dakota, and Omaha, Nebraska.

The year 1955 marked a turning point in radio. A number of well-known radio network shows ended, including *The Jack Benny Program,* which had begun in 1932; *The Lone Ranger,* which began in 1933; *Lux Radio Theatre,* begun in 1934; *The Roy Rogers Show,* begun in 1944; *Sergeant Preston of the Yukon,* begun in 1947; *The Hallmark Hall of Fame,* begun in 1948; and *The Whistler,* begun in 1947. The importance of network radio was diminished as sponsors and programs shifted over to television. The economics of broadcasting dictated a change in programming. The high-dollar national sponsors moved over to TV for the national audience, making radio increasingly a local rather than a national medium. Further, the shift in national sponsors precipitated a drop in income, and with that loss radio could no longer afford to produce live shows or keep a staff band on the payroll. More and more radio substituted records for live shows. And although radio had played records on the air since before World War II, after 1955 the airwaves were dominated by records playing.

At this time there was also a huge shift in the tastes of the population. In 1955 Bill Haley's recording of "Rock Around the Clock" reached number one, marking the official beginning of the rock and roll era. The next year Elvis Presley sold 10 million records, with teenagers becoming the dominant record market. This shift in taste cost the major labels a great deal. Until 1955 the six major record labels dominated the pop music charts; however, in 1956 small, independent labels that had invested in rhythm and blues, when the major labels stuck with white pop singers like Perry Como and Eddie Fisher, usurped the big labels' power. By the end of 1956 twenty-five different labels had hits in the Top 50 recordings.

In 1951 Patti Page sold 2.2 million copies of her recording of "The Tennessee Waltz," and Nashville was on top of the world. A number of songs from country music songwriters at Nashville publishing companies were recorded by pop acts. The biggest single beneficiary was the publisher Acuff-Rose and their songwriter Hank Williams, who had hits recorded by Tony Bennett, Jo Stafford, and Rosemary Clooney. In 1951 more than a third of the sales of recordings were country. Tennessee Ernie Ford, Red Foley, Ernest Tubb, Hank Williams, and Little Jimmy Dickens all averaged about 750,000 in sales per release, and Eddy Arnold's record sales topped a million for each release. At Columbia Records about 40 percent of sales were to the country market, and at Decca about half of their sales were attributed to country.

But in 1956 the bottom fell out. Elvis Presley was signed in Nashville and was originally considered a country artist, but his success quickly transcended the country music field. Other young performers—such as the Everly Brothers, Carl Perkins, Jerry Lee Lewis, and other rockabilly pioneers—also had roots in country, but, again, their appeal went beyond the traditional country music audience. In 1958 the new category "Rock and Roll" was created by the trade magazines to track airplay and sales for this new style of music.

From a business perspective, rock and roll was fueled by the growth of independent labels that recorded music (primarily rhythm and blues) that the major labels were not. The small labels were aided by AM radio, which had shifted over to records from live talent and was now playing the new music. Because the signals for AM reached long distances at night, bouncing off the ionosphere, the sounds of a big city could penetrate rural and small-town areas. The arbiters of taste may have wanted to keep rock and roll out of their small towns—and, in many instances, did keep it off their local radio stations—but they could not keep the music off of radios tuned into distant signals.

As radio became local instead of national, it had to better target a market. For most of its history radio had presented a smorgasbord of programs to appeal to a broad cross-section of the American listening public. But television replaced radio as the medium for the masses, and radio increasingly had to find an audience that television was not reaching. The audience that radio found in 1956–58 was made up of teenagers who wanted to hear rock and roll and rhythm and blues records.

Many young country performers moved into rock and roll, taking with them the young white working-class audience. Older country artists, or those uncomfortable with the new sound and new audience, could not or would not make the shift to rock and roll. Radio increasingly abandoned country music in favor of rock or rhythm and blues music, and thus country music was left without significant exposure to the mass audience. Jukeboxes had become less important than radio, and even they were loading up their machines with rock and roll records, and television was not particularly interested in country, although there were a few shows on the air (most significantly *The Ozark Jubilee*).

The Nashville country music community reacted by forming the Country Music Association (CMA) in 1958 from the remains of the Country and Western Disc Jockeys Association, which had all but disbanded. A key part of the game plan for the CMA was to appeal to advertising agencies and sponsors to buy ads on country radio and make programming country music profitable. They felt that if there was money, then programming would follow. To this extent they were incredibly successful.

In their first official survey of country radio in 1961, the CMA discovered only eighty-one stations playing country music full time. However, through their efforts the number of country stations began to show a steady increase throughout the 1960s and there was more country music exposure on television, which resulted in growth in country music recordings and sales through its increased exposure on radio and TV. Those who marketed and produced country music concentrated on creating a smoother sound for an adult population—"the Nashville Sound"—that could appeal to the pop music markets as country music pursued "crossovers," recordings that could appear on both the pop and country radio formats (and charts). If crossover success could be achieved, then big sales could result; simply sticking to the country music market meant limited sales. Some of the big crossover artists who enjoyed the benefits of this move were Eddy Arnold, Patsy Cline, Jim Reeves, Johnny Cash, and Roger Miller.

This movement toward "the Nashville Sound" and the work by the Country Music Association to get country music on radio would lead to country music's emergence as the music of the middle class, transcending its working-class roots but, at the same time, keeping that audience. Baseball had made this move by the early 1960s, becoming the sport of the American middle class.

In terms of broadcasting, country music had an advantage over baseball because country music's major medium was radio. As the networks shifted their attention to television, radio was left to carve a separate niche. They did this by using recordings on the air and concentrating on a particular kind of music. Unlike baseball, country music was not seasonal, and could be broadcast year-round, twenty-four-hours a day, while baseball was limited to seasons and game times. Thus, whereas country music thrived on radio, that medium became less important for national exposure for baseball, though it continued to be important because it usually broadcast *all* the games while local television only broadcast selected games. And so while the general audience increasingly sat in front of a television at night with the radio off, baseball lost much of its audience to popular TV shows.

10

Baseball and Country Music in a Changing World

The challenge to both baseball and country music during the 1950s and 1960s was how to appeal to a core audience, the white middle class, without losing the white working class. Added to this was the problem of how each industry could operate with a profit.

Baseball looked at diversity of players as a way of attracting new fans. When a team had a great Italian ballplayer like Joe DiMaggio or a great Jewish ballplayer like Hank Greenberg, the owner knew there would be a host of Italian or Jewish fans who would pay to see the game. But, at the same time, they worried that having too many ethnic ballplayers and fans would make the white Protestants in the stands uncomfortable at the ballpark. The value of black ballplayers wasn't just in their contribution on the field but in their tickets sales.

Branch Rickey knew the Negro leagues attracted large numbers of paying customers, and he wanted some of that money to go to the Brooklyn Dodgers and into his own pockets. He did have a commitment to integrating baseball, and he saw an injustice he wanted to remedy, but Rickey's motives were not totally altruistic.

As the population shifted from rural to urban and then out to the suburbs, the white audience increasingly moved away from the cities. This trend was exacerbated by the growth of suburban housing developments after World War II as well as by the government financing of new homes for veterans. Thus the housing in cities depreciated, allowing blacks—who had lower incomes—to increasingly move to cities. In 1950 the white urban dweller accounted for 51 percent of the city population; by the end of that decade the figure was down to 39 percent. As whites moved out and lower-income blacks moved in, increasingly these parks were located in parts of town that were predominantly black, and white fans were reluctant to venture into the area where the ballpark was located. The end result was a shift to baseball stadiums being built outside of cities.

There were several factors during the 1950s that would eventually lead to a decline in baseball's popularity from the mid-1960s on. The G.I. Bill provided World War II veterans with the opportunity to go to college; this resulted in many more lower- and middle-class Americans getting college educations. As more and more Americans attended college, college sports became increasingly popular. And while baseball was a game that developed on sandlots and semi-pro leagues, basketball and football were played by colleges. So as professional basketball and football leagues developed in the 1950s they had a larger pool of talent to draw from and a larger fan base for their games.

Another factor is directly related to the growth of the suburbs. With the suburbs came the development of Little League baseball, which was increasingly rooted in the suburbs and meant a large number of white children played. With the absence of Little League teams in the inner cities, basketball courts, which were less expensive and required less space, were built on playgrounds and in parks. High schools developed their basketball and football programs because it was easier to attract a crowd to these events than for baseball games. Basketball games were held in the evenings indoors during the winter when there was less competition for a young person's time. Football games, since they were fewer in number, became an "event" and thus it was easier to attract a crowd for five "events" during the fall (a high school team usually played ten games, five at home) than baseball, which was played in the summer when school was out and which had a long season. Thus, young athletes could play before a large, enthusiastic crowd (and receive press coverage) if they played basketball or football but faced only a sparse crowd in the stands for baseball games. Also, as the leisure time and habits of Americans grew, summers were increasingly seen as the time to have "fun," and a variety of activities became available that competed with baseball.

The incentives for a young athlete to devote himself to basketball or football grew during the 1960s and 1970s. College scholarships were made available to the most gifted athletes, and if they played in college they could be assured of large enthusiastic crowds as well as press—sometimes even national—attention. Star players could go straight into the National Basketball Association or the National Football League after having served their apprenticeship in college. Baseball players, however, had to spend years in the minor leagues, playing before sparse crowds with little financial incentive, before they got a shot at the majors. And while a college basketball or football player might be seen on national television, a minor league ballplayer would not. With the fame came money, so a young athlete looking at a career in sports would quickly conclude that his future lay with basketball or football, not baseball.

Beginning in the 1950s colleges began to replace the minor league system as a source of baseball talent. While the minors were declining, college baseball programs were growing. One problem was that colleges did not play as many games as the minor leagues, and ballplayers had to attend classes and other activities that took their minds off baseball. Another "problem" was that colleges gave players education and independence, which meant they were less likely to accept the owner's way of doing business as "that's just the way it is." This became increasingly apparent in the 1960s and 1970s as baseball players discarded the clean-cut, All-American image in favor of long hair, beards, and flashy outfits. Education also gave baseball players other options. No longer did a young man either play baseball or work at manual labor; with a college degree they could have a good job outside or after baseball.

Country music, too, was affected by the large number of young people attending college. Although artists often did not go to college, executives did. Country music executives who handled the marketing and sales of this music were increasingly college educated; they found the old-fashioned haphazard ways of doing business unacceptable to the modern world. This new breed of industry manager began pushing artists away from the rural image and audience and toward a more cosmopolitan look and sound. "The Nashville Sound" was created so that country music could appeal to the suburban middle class, exchanging the twangs and rhinestone suits for smooth-voiced singers dressed in sports coats or tuxes. This reflected the move of the country music audience to the suburbs, which was increasingly populated by people who did not have a rural heritage of their own, although their parents may have been raised on farms. This new generation would demand a country music that dealt with life's problems through intelligent, well-crafted songs.

11

Baseball and Country Music's Troubled Times

The years 1945–65 are a study in contrasts for both country music and baseball. Some look back on these years as a golden age for both baseball and country music. In baseball it was the time of superstars Mickey Mantle, Willie Mays, Duke Snider, Bob Feller, Stan Musial, Roy Campanella, Jackie Robinson, Ted Kluszewski, Yogi Berra, Nellie Fox, Luis Aparicio, Eddie Matthews, Henry Aaron, Ken Boyer, George Kell, Ernie Banks, Phil Rizzuto, Pee Wee Reese, Ted Williams, Frank Robinson, Richie Ashburn, Al Kaline, Warren Spahn, Whitey Ford, Robin Roberts, Bob Lemon, and Early Wynn. For country music it was the era of Hank Williams, Eddy Arnold, Webb Pierce, Kitty Wells, Lefty Frizzell, Hank Snow, Red Foley, Ernest Tubb, Hank Thompson, Jim Reeves, Marty Robbins,

Ray Price, George Jones, and Tennessee Ernie Ford. On the field and on the record, many argue, baseball and country music never had it better.

But in terms of *business,* both baseball and country music suffered great losses during this period. Baseball had the same teams in the same cites for fifty years, from 1903 to 1953. That changed, however, when the Boston Braves moved to Milwaukee in 1953. The following year the Browns moved to Baltimore and became the Orioles, and in 1955 the Athletics moved from Philadelphia to Kansas City. Then, in 1958, two New York teams—the Giants and Dodgers—moved to California. It was a massive realignment of the sport and indicative of both the allure of new markets and the realization that baseball was not terribly profitable during this period. The Washington Senators moved to Minnesota and became the Minnesota Twins in 1961. The California Angels (then called the Los Angeles Angels) were an American League expansion team in 1961, while a "new" Washington Senators expansion team replaced the team that had departed. In 1962 the New York Mets and the Houston Colt 45's (later named the Astros) joined the major leagues.

The first step in the major leagues arriving on the West Coast was made in 1921 when William K. Wrigley, majority stockholder in the Chicago Cubs, purchased the Los Angeles Angels in the Pacific Coast League. The Angels remained a farm club of the Cubs through the 1956 season. In February 1957 the Cubs sold the Angels to Walter O'Malley, owner of the Brooklyn Dodgers for $3 million. In addition, the Cubs got the Dodger's Texas League farm club in Fort Worth, Texas. O'Malley was dissatisfied with Ebbet's Field in Brooklyn, which was located in the inner city with no room to expand and only limited parking. O'Malley (as well as other major league owners) was well aware of the potential for baseball on the West Coast, evidenced by the success of the Pacific Coast League. Now that he had ownership in a Pacific Coast League franchise, O'Malley could move his club to Los Angeles, which he did for the 1958 season.

In the fall of 1957 it was obvious that the Giants and Dodgers were going to move West, so the Pacific Coast League directors rearranged the league: the Angels would move to Spokane and the Seals would move to Phoenix. Bob Cobb, president of the Hollywood Stars, reluctantly sold his franchise to interests in Salt Lake City, so the Dodgers had the Los Angeles market to themselves from 1958 to 1960. But the major leagues decided to expand for the 1961 season, and the American League wanted a franchise in Los Angeles. Bill Veeck and Hank Greenberg were set to get the L.A. franchise, but O'Malley demanded money because his territory was being "invaded." Veeck and Greenberg balked at the price. This left the L.A. franchise somewhat up for grabs.

Gene Autry's radio station, KMPC, had the rights to broadcast the Dodgers' games, and Autry had regular-season box seats. But at the end of 1960 O'Malley decided to not renew his agreement with Autry's station, so Autry was left with no baseball games to broadcast. This led him to approach Veeck and Greenberg, since he was aware of the negotiations between O'Malley and the prospective owners of the Angels. When the negotiations broke down, Autry called Joe Cronin, the American League president. Autry had always loved baseball and welcomed major league baseball players backstage during his performances. In Boston Autry had originally met Red Sox player-manager Cronin backstage after a performance and given cowboy hats to some children with Cronin. Here was a major star with a clean-cut All-American image, a hero to many baseball players, fans, and executives, checking into the American League franchise. The deal was soon struck. From 1961 until his death in 1998, Gene Autry owned the Los Angeles (later Anaheim) Angels, although he sold 25 percent of the Angels to the Walt Disney Corporation in 1996 and gave up day-to-day management of the team.

Another interesting link between baseball and country music occurred in the spring of 1962 at the Angels spring training camp. In the camp was Charley Pride, who began his baseball career with the Memphis Red Sox in the Negro American League as a pitcher under manager Homer "Goose" Curry. From Memphis Pride joined an all-Negro team in the Iowa State League and then went back to Memphis, where he pitched and played the outfield. During road trips Pride often sang on the bus country songs by Hank Williams and Roy Acuff.

Pride signed with the New York Yankees farm team in Boise, Idaho, a Class C team, but was sent to Fond du Lac, Wisconsin, because of a sore arm. The sore arm was a problem; he returned to Memphis and then bounced around to the Louisville Clippers, Birmingham Black Barons, the El Paso Kings, and a team in Nogales, Mexico, before he rejoined the Memphis Red Sox for the 1956 season. He cracked a bone in his elbow while pitching, which caused scouts from the Brooklyn Dodgers and St. Louis Cardinals to pass on him. Determined to have a career in baseball, Pride worked on a knuckleball and played with a group of Negro League All-Stars that toured the South playing exhibition games against the Willie Mays All-Stars. While touring with this team Pride played against Elston Howard, Monte Irvin, Gene Baker, Hank Aaron, Lew Burdette, Warren Spahn, and Willie Mays.

After a stint in the army, where he served in the Special Services and played on the baseball team for Fort Carson in Colorado, he returned to the Memphis Red Sox before joining the Missoula (Montana) Timberjacks in the Pioneer League in the spring of 1960. When he was cut from the team, twenty-three-year-old Pride joined the East Helena Smelterites for the 1961 season, working for the American Smelting and Refining Company while playing for the company team.

After the games he sang in bars and managed to get a job singing at the White Mill Bar in Helena, Montana.

Pride sent a letter with some press clippings to Fred Haney, general manager of the Angels, requesting a tryout for the 1962 season. Manager Bill Rigney replied that if he could make it to spring training in Palm Springs, California, on March 1, they would take a look at him. But after two weeks the pitching coach took him aside and told him, "Charley, you just don't have a major league pitching arm. We're going to have to let you go." Pride immediately set out to find Gene Autry, who was eating lunch at the hotel. There he begged Autry to intervene. Autry replied that he did not run the team; manager Bill Rigney made those decisions. Dejected, Pride left camp and returned to Montana.

The next season Pride went to the spring training camp for the New York Mets, hoping for a tryout. But manager Casey Stengel would not even let him on the field; dejected, Pride left the camp and decided to stop in Nashville before he returned to Montana. Country star Red Sovine had heard Pride sing in Montana and offered to help him if he came to Nashville. Pride called Sovine, who arranged an audition, which led to Charley Pride being signed to RCA Records and becoming a country music superstar.

A number of minor leagues collapsed in the 1955–65 period. The two major cities in the Pacific Coast

League, San Francisco and Los Angeles, lost their franchises. By 1960 the Nashville Vols "were struggling to make the 100,000 mark."[1] The Southern Association was dead by 1962 although the Vols played the 1963 season in the South Atlantic League. At the end of the 1963 season, baseball was gone from Nashville. The Sulphur Dell was torn down and the property sold; attendance had declined from 270,000 in 1948 to less than 55,000. By this time the club was owned by 4,876 fans, headed up by a group of investors that included country star Eddy Arnold. The fans had each invested five dollars or more to keep baseball in Nashville, but the club could not survive. The Southern Association and the South Atlantic League reformed in 1964 as the Southern League, but Nashville did not have a team in that league. Indeed, minor league baseball would not return to Nashville for fifteen years.

The major leagues attempted to help the minors by combining the Class AA and A Leagues into a new Class AA, while the Class B, C, and D circuits became Class A. For freshmen prospects a Rookie League was created; AAA baseball remained unchanged. Every major league team would have one Class AAA affiliate, one AA affiliate, three Class A, and one Rookie League affiliate. The major league club would provide a manager for each of its minor league teams, cover spring training expenses, and reimburse the minors teams for the players' salaries. A draft was also instituted, letting major league teams claim "ownership" of minor league players. This meant that minor league teams no longer operated independently but were part of the major league organization. Thus, the idea that a minor league team could field former major leaguers or have a solid core of players through the year gave way to the concept of the minors developing players for the majors. With the constant shuffling of players in and out of a minor league team, it was difficult to keep a fan base.

While major league baseball was expanding, country music was consolidating and contracting, increasingly centering its activities in Nashville. Before World War II there was no real "center" for country music, though there were vibrant scenes in Hollywood, Chicago, Dallas, and Atlanta. But as *The Grand Ole Opry* emerged as the major radio program for country music by virtue of the talent it attracted as well as the range of its signal and the simple fact that it stayed on the air while other country music shows did not, executives emerged from the Opry's ranks to form important business companies. Also, other entrepreneurs with connections to the Opry began companies that would eventually flourish.

The first, most important company outside the Grand Ole Opry was Acuff-Rose Publishing Company, formed by Roy Acuff and Fred Rose. The next important company was the booking agency formed by Jim Denny, the former manager of the Grand Ole Opry who was fired in 1956 because of his outside business interests. Also in 1956 Tree Publishing, formed by

WSM executive Jack Stapp, published Elvis Presley's hit "Heartbreak Hotel" and became a major publishing firm, along with Jim Denny's Cedarwood. The major record labels were increasingly recording country artists in Nashville because of the proliferation of studios, most notably the one formed by Owen Bradley on 16th Avenue South, an area that would later become known as "Music Row."

The establishment of an office and studio by RCA Victor in 1955, as well as offices established by record labels Columbia, Capitol, Mercury, and Decca, all led the country music industry to be increasingly centered in Nashville. The formation of the Country Music Association at the end of 1958 as a "chamber of commerce" for country music and the establishment of the Country Music Hall of Fame in 1961 and its opening in 1967 were also major reasons why Nashville emerged as the mecca for country music.

However, despite this growth of both industries, country music and baseball ran into major roadblocks during the 1950s; for baseball it was television, for country music it was rock and roll. Baseball did not adapt well to television. One problem was that fans and owners have always seen the game being set in pastoral settings in the middle of an urban America. G. Edward White, in *Creating the National Pastime,* notes, "Baseball grew up with America's cities, its teams becoming a focus of civic pride and energy. At the same time baseball's fields and parks, the leisurely pace of the game, and its being an outdoor, daytime spectacle invoked rural and pastoral associations that were particularly evocative to a generation of Americans confronting an increasing urbanization in an industrializing environment."2

Television does not do justice to baseball; fans need to see a large field to appreciate the game. Cameras zero in on a small area of action—which is why football and basketball are better television sports. Baseball tends to concentrate on the pitcher and hitter, integral parts of the game, for sure, but this concentration ignores the expansive field on which they play. Also, baseball is a slower paced game (although this slowness has been exacerbated in recent years), and it is difficult for fans to sit in front of a television and tolerate all the time it takes for the batter to get set, the pitcher to get ready, and the pitch to be made—most of which are not hit.

For country music the emergence of rock and roll and Elvis Presley in 1956 almost dealt a death blow to the industry. The young white audience wanted to see rock and roll performers who were young and attractive. That meant that the demand for live appearances for country music performers virtually disappeared overnight. They could not attract the crowds that rock and roll could, so promoters and bookers, whose livelihoods depended on paying customers, booked rock and roll instead of country music.

Radio stations also dropped country music and played rock and roll instead, and television furthered the trend as well. Before TV radio was dominated by the networks, which programmed a number of live shows. However, as viewers shifted to television, the advertising dollars quickly followed, and soon radio stations could not afford to hire live talent. Increasingly disk jockeys played records instead of booking live acts. This coincided with the rock and roll revolution, whose roots can be traced back to the increasing popularity of rhythm and blues after World War II.

In many ways, what Jackie Robinson was to baseball, Elvis Presley was to the music industry; both shook up the existing order in their respective fields. Jackie Robinson led the integration of baseball, while Elvis, although he was white, led the integration of pop music. A number of talented black ball players and musical artists followed their lead and entered the mainstream, but the mainstream was not comfortable with all the developments. The level of play was raised, but so was the level of unease. For baseball this marked the beginning of an integrated sport; for country music it did not. Country music remained white, and rock and roll—which began with southern boys singing "black music"—became the first really integrated music in America. In doing so, rock and roll left country music behind and forged an identity of its own.

While it is easy to blame the southern tradition in country music and the fact that this music is rooted in the South for the lack of full racial integration in the industry, the explanation must go deeper. In baseball people root for a *team,* and a player is only one of nine on the field. People still bought tickets to see the game, and they could still root for the Dodgers even if they didn't like the fact that Jackie Robinson was playing. But in country music the performer is *the* focal point for the crowd; if the customer doesn't like the focal point, he won't buy tickets for the show.

Actually, country music was integrated *before* baseball. DeFord Bailey, an African American harmonica player, was a star on the early Grand Ole Opry. Blacks also played in string bands during the early recording years, in groups like Taylor's Kentucky Boys, the Georgia Yellow Hammers, the James Cole String Band, and the Mississippi Sheiks. Early radio listeners could not see the musicians who were performing what sounded like early "hillbilly" music string bands. Hudie Ledbetter, better known as Leadbelly, essentially played "country" music, but the recording labels isolated the music according to race; so since Leadbelly was a black performer, his music was called "blues."[3]

The problem was not the music itself but the audience, and the record companies targeted the rural white and black audiences separately. Although white customers bought records by black performers, and vice versa, and black and white musicians influenced each other, the record companies put the music in different categories in order to differentiate the buyers of the records. While the audiences were primarily segregated as they were listening, the fact remains that whites listened to music by black musicians and blacks listened to music by white musicians.

Baseball integrated slowly in the early years, and teams were careful not to have too many black players (and some teams had none). The concern, again, was the audience. While both whites and blacks might love and follow a baseball team, the owners did not want them sitting too close together for fear of offending—and losing—the core white audience that might feel intimidated and stop buying tickets if too many blacks were seated close by.

At the same time Elvis was hitting big in America, television was also coming into its own. What this meant for radio, which lost the middle-class audience to television, was that its future lay in attracting with rock and roll a new audience of teenagers and youth. This excluded country music, which in the mid-1950s remained the music of the older white working class.

Although in many ways Elvis Presley and Jackie Robinson played parallel roles, if Elvis should be compared to anyone in baseball during the 1950s it would be to Mickey Mantle. In 1956, when Elvis sold 10 million records, Mantle won the Triple Crown, leading the American League in batting average (.353), home runs (52), and RBIs (130). Both dominated their fields and were made heroes by the youth of America. Both were born during the Great Depression—Mantle on

October 20, 1931, and Elvis on January 8, 1935—and were from areas hit hard by the times, Mantle from Oklahoma and Elvis from Mississippi. They both came of age when the young baby boomers, born after World War II, were looking to baseball and music for heroes. Elvis and Mantle both filled those roles. For a generation raised believing they could be anything they wanted to be, Elvis and Mickey Mantle set the standard for what a young boy growing up in the late 1950s dreamed of becoming.

12

Baseball and Country Music on TV

Stage Two

By 1960 the television set was firmly established as an essential and central piece of furniture in American homes. It was the medium with the greatest mass appeal, and both baseball and country music faced a common problem: how to appeal to the television audience. Neither succeeded very well, and the story of the struggle by both baseball and country music to reach a large, national audience revolves around their exposure on television. Country music had a slight advantage in that it received its major exposure on the radio. While baseball also received exposure on radio, as more and more games were played at night in order to attract fans to the ballpark after work, the broadcasts suffered because they now had to compete with television programming.

Also, baseball games were played only at certain times; country music could be played around the clock. Thus country music made it back onto the airwaves while baseball did not.

The longest-running country music TV show—and the one that has received the most criticism for stigmatizing country music with stereotypes it has yet to shake—began on June 15, 1969. *Hee Haw* featured top country acts but had a distinctly yokel feel. Hosted by Roy Clark and Buck Owens, the show ran on the CBS network until 1971 when it went into syndication.

In many ways *Hee Haw* was a throwback to country music from a bygone era. The radio barn dances of the 1940s featured big casts and rube comedy and played up the hayseed image. But as country music emerged from the 1950s it increasingly moved away from the hick image toward one with a more suburban appeal. Rhinestone suits replaced bib overalls, and comedy was deemphasized. In TV the emergence of the "star" performer meant that the casts were much smaller and the old barn dance format was out. Also, throughout the 1950s and 1960s country music sought to move uptown, present a more dignified and respectable image, and move away from the traditional stereotype of blue-collar hicks. But *Hee Haw* had a huge cast, dressed their regulars in bib overalls, and used old vaudeville and barn dance routines in their comedy skits. It was immensely popular, both to the enjoyment and chagrin of the country music establishment. On the one hand it proved the immense national appeal of country music, but on the other hand it saddled country music with an image it had been trying to deny and escape: country bumpkins down on the farm. *Hee Haw* producers argued that it was all just good clean fun and booked older acts who were no longer played on radio.

The most popular country music show on television during the 1970s and 1980s was *The Country Music Association's Awards Show,* which originated in Nashville and, broadcast each fall, served to boost country music on TV. Another popular awards show was *The Academy of Country Music Awards,* which originated in Los Angeles and was broadcast each spring. But the history of country music on TV was rewritten in March 1983 when the Nashville Network and Country Music Television went on the air. This arrival of country music on cable television coincided with the rise of cable television in the United States. Cable television helped country music by bringing the artists directly into American homes via Country Music Television (CMT) and the Nashville Network (TNN), thus freeing country music from the national networks who presented country music sparingly or, when they did, altered to fit stereotypes perpetuated by New York and Los Angeles TV executives.

Cable television also helped baseball, which had suffered a loss of viewership in the 1970s to football. This can in part be attributed to *Monday Night Football,* which began in the fall of 1970. The sport of football was made for television. First, the action is centered on one area of the field, so the television camera can focus more readily on the plays. But, more important, football is played in the fall and winter, when TV viewing peaks; baseball is played in the spring and summer, when TV viewing is at its lowest. Also, during the 1970s football teams only played once a week, or fourteen times a season, while baseball's major league season is 162 games. But cable gave fans a steady diet of baseball, appealing to core fans without having to attract the big numbers from a diverse audience. The "superstations" in Chicago and Atlanta made national teams of the Cubs and Braves, and ESPN's sports fans are happy to watch a variety of teams throughout the season. Like country music, baseball is on television on its own terms, appealing to baseball or sports fans instead of trying to reach a broad, mass audience, and this has helped the game. No longer do baseball or country music have to be all things to all people; now they can be what they are, and the fans are happier for it.

Still, the networks know that there are huge audiences for country music and baseball each year for such special events as *The Country Music Association's Awards Show* and the World Series—both held in the fall. While baseball does not pull big numbers throughout the summer for TV networks, it certainly attracts a large audience for events like the All-Star Game, division playoffs, and World Series—proof positive that the American public has not totally abandoned baseball.

And while country music also does not draw big TV ratings week in and week out, the big awards show is consistently one of the top-rated shows on network TV each year, proving the appeal of this music to a large, national audience.

Conclusion

Nothing is more quintessentially American than baseball and country music. Each had its roots in England—the games of rounders and cricket for baseball and the British folk songs for country music—but each was developed in the United States during the nineteenth century. Each has received broad international exposure, but neither has really been exported successfully around the globe. True, the Japanese play baseball and country music is heard around the world, but neither has had the global impact of soccer or rock and roll.

During the twentieth century both baseball and country music expanded into truly national entertainment. Until 1953 there were sixteen major league teams in ten cities; none of these cities was further south than Washington, D.C., or further west than St. Louis. At the start of the 2000 season there were thirty major league teams in twenty-four cities; the South and the Southwest, both strongholds for country music, have major league teams in Los Angeles, Houston, Dallas-Fort Worth, Phoenix, Miami, Tampa Bay, Kansas City, Oakland, San Francisco, San Diego, Atlanta, and Denver. Of the original ten cities only one, Washington, D.C., does not have a major league baseball team, but that market is served by the Baltimore ball club, located about forty miles from old Griffith Stadium, the Senators old ballpark.

Country music was a regional music before World War II, limited to the South, but since the war it has become a national music, with country music radio stations now broadcasting from all over the country. And although major league baseball was long considered our national sport, until 1958 it was geographically "regional": if the country were divided into quarters, only the top-right quarter had major league teams.

The link between baseball and Nashville became stronger when, in 1978, Nashville became home to a AA club in the Southern League, the Nashville Sounds. It is a tribute to the connection between baseball and country music that when baseball came back to Nashville the name of the ball club was not the Vols, with its Civil War association, but was connected to the country music industry. Leading the way to bring baseball back to Nashville was a group of investors led by Larry Schmittou, a former baseball coach at Vanderbilt. A new ballpark was built—Greer Stadium—only about a mile or so from Music Row. Schmittou had gone to the 1977 winter baseball meetings attempting to get a AAA ball club in the American Association; instead, they landed a AA club in the Southern League and worked out details with Southern League president Billy Hitchcock.

By this time Nashville was thirsty for baseball. The Sounds led the Southern League in attendance every season from 1978 to 1984. They won two league titles (1979 and 1982) and were the most successful franchise in the Southern League in terms of paying customers during this period. In 1985 Nashville became a AAA club with the American Association, keeping the name Nashville Sounds.

The Sounds generated a great deal of interest within the country music community, and several country artists, including Conway Twitty and the Oak Ridge Boys' singer Richard Sterban, were investors in the ball club. Country artists came to the game, sang the national anthem, and wrote songs about baseball, including "I Saw It All on My Radio," recorded by Lionel Cartwright, and "Cheap Seats," a hit for the group Alabama.

As baseball and country music developed into big business, three basic major revenue streams developed for each. The first was paid attendance at either ballgames or concerts. The second was money generated from broadcasting on radio and TV. And third was the sale of "product," which for country music meant compact discs and cassettes and for baseball meant the sale of merchandise with team logos. At major league games it is not unusual to hear country songs coming out of the speakers between innings ("Thank God I'm a Country Boy" by John Denver is regularly played at Baltimore Orioles games) or see a country music star sing the national anthem on a televised game. And in Nashville's country music circles the discussion of baseball is a common topic. It is not unusual to see fans at a baseball game wearing a t-shirt with a country star's picture and name on it or at country music concerts to see fans in baseball caps from major league teams.

Both country music and baseball have benefited from public financing through the years—a recognition from local governments of their importance. When the early stadiums were torn down—beginning with Ebbets Field in Brooklyn in 1960 and followed by the Polo Grounds in New York, Griffith Stadium in Washington, Sportsman's Park in St. Louis, Forbes Field in Pittsburgh, Crosley Field in Cincinnati, and Shibe Park in Philadelphia—they were replaced with stadiums built through public financing. Of all the baseball parks built since the 1960s began only one—Dodger Stadium in Los Angeles—was built with private funds. Country music has also benefited from the concert arenas, erected with public funds, that provide large venues for fans to see the artists. The federal government's financing of the interstate highway system has also benefited country music artists, who travel all over the country in large buses unsuited to two-lane highways. These same interstates regularly bring baseball fans from a two-hundred-mile radius to see major league baseball games.

In the future of baseball and country music there is a large potential market within the Latino population. During the World War II years the major leagues signed a number of Latin American players. The Washington Senators under owner Clark Griffith was the leading club in signing Latin players, with seven on the twenty-five-man roster in 1944. In addition to their talent, Latin players were also "cheaper," playing for less money, and thus a club could keep its payroll down.

By the 1997 season about 30 percent of all major league players were Latinos, and in 1996 some major league games were played in Monterrey, Mexico, when the San Diego Padres had to find a place to play while their stadium was being repaired. The large number of enthusiastic fans—bolstered by the fact that Mexican star Fernando Valenzuela was pitching for the Padres in the first game of that series—proved that the Latin market was a strong one for baseball. An advantage of the Latin market is that baseball is played year-round in Mexico, Venezuela, and the Caribbean. For years major leaguers have played winter ball there and increasingly have seen it as a source for new talent. The Dominican Republic produces more major league baseball players per square mile than anywhere else in the world.

For country music, the large number of Latinos in Texas has produced a "Tejano" music that is appealing to country fans, and commercial country music has always had an appeal to Hispanics in the Southwest. During the 1970s Johnny Rodriguez and Freddy Fender became country music stars singing in both Spanish and English, and in the 1990s the major recording labels marketed acts like Rick Trevino and Emilio to the Hispanic as well as traditional country audience. Latinos have also influenced country music in the colorful costumes worn by country stars. The fancy rhinestone suits are a product of the Spanish influence in southern California. The Spanish guitar has also had a major impact on country music, and Latino influences will continue to be a part of country music in the future.

Baseball and country music continue to ride a wave of popularity. On the downside, the baseball players' strike in 1994, which led to the cancellation of the World Series that year, left a sour taste in the mouths of many Americans, leaving many to call themselves "former baseball fans." But the home run battle between Mark McGwire and Sammy Sosa and Cal Ripken's consecutive game streak in 1998 did bring some fans back.

Similarly, country music lost many in its core audience during the latter half of the 1990s when a youth movement swept the scene. These young performers, mostly raised on rock, attracted big money and big crowds and moved the music away from its core audience of white working-class Americans. By the end of the 1990s country music had lost favor with much of its older audience (leaving many to call themselves "former country music fans") and was not gaining many new young converts.

The connection between baseball and country music was reinforced during the 1999 and 2000 spring training seasons, when country music's biggest star, Garth Brooks, joined a major league team to chase a dream. Even though Brooks's dream of country music stardom had come true beyond his wildest imagination, the dream of being a major league baseball player still lingered unfulfilled. During the 1999 spring training season, Brooks worked out with the San Diego Padres, and during the 2000 spring training season he wore a New York Mets uniform. Although baseball taught Garth Brooks some lessons (mainly how difficult it is to become a major league athlete in your late thirties and hit a ninety-mile-an-hour baseball), Garth taught baseball a few things, too. He reminded them of the importance of connecting with fans, signing autographs for hours, posing for pictures, and allowing contact with an "audience." He also noted an essential difference between baseball and country music: in performing you want to reach out to your audience and make a connection in order to have a successful show; in baseball you need to isolate yourself from the crowd in order to concentrate on the tasks at hand.

Perhaps the most important contribution baseball and country music make to America is summed up in two quotes. Gene Autry, talking about his early dream of playing baseball, said, "To play baseball, to reach the big leagues, that was the great national escape of my boyhood, especially for the poor ones looking for a way to get off the farm."[1] And Sparky Anderson, former manager of the Cincinnati Reds and Detroit Tigers, said, "This game has taken a lot of guys over the years, who would have had to work in factories and gas stations, and made them prominent people. . . . In this business you can walk into a room with millionaires, doctors, professional people and get more attention than they get."[2] Both baseball and country music have taken people who were born without social status, money, and connections but with great talent and allowed them to rise to the top and become heroes. Coming from a working-class background and ending up on top of the world is the American dream. Baseball and country music both deliver that dream, and you can't get more American than that.

Notes

Bibliographical Essay

Bibliography

Index

Notes

Introduction

1. Geoffrey Ward and Ken Burns, *Baseball: An Illustrated History*, xvii.

Chapter 1. The Early Years

1. Edward G. White, *Creating the National Pastime: Baseball Transforms Itself, 1903–1953*, 4.

2. Charles C. Alexander *Our Game: An American Baseball History*, 18.

3. Bill Malone, *Singing Cowboys and Musical Mountaineers: Southern Culture and the Roots of Country Music*. This book discusses this issue at length.

4. White, *Creating the National Pastime*, 23.

Chapter 2. Radio and Electricity

1. Russell Sanjek, *American Popular Music and Its Business: The First Four Hundred Years*, 218.

Chapter 3. Country Music and Baseball in America

1. "First Baseball Game Here Was in Late Sixties," *Nashville Banner*, Oct. 30, 1932.

2. "Base Ball," *Nashville Dispatch,* Aug. 1, 1866, displayed in the Nashville Room, Nashville Public Library.

3. "Base Ball," *Nashville Dispatch,* Aug. 17, 1866, displayed in the Nashville Room, Nashville Public Library.

4. Grantland Rice, "Base Ball's Boom in Dixie," *The Taylor-Trotwood Magazine,* May 1910.

5. Ibid.

6. Charles K. Wolfe, *Tennessee Strings: The Story of Country Music in Tennessee,* chap. 3.

7. Fred Russell, "Memories Linger of Nashville's Unique Ball Park, Sulphur Dell," *Nashville Banner,* Mar. 18, 1988.

8. Alexander, *Our Game,* 94, 14, 94, 4, 4, 95.

9. Bill James, *The Politics of Glory: How Baseball's Hall of Fame Really Works,* 2, 5.

Chapter 4. War Clouds Gather

1. Advertisement, *Billboard Magazine,* Apr. 30, 1949, 36.

2. Bill Monroe, *Bill Monroe's Blue Grass Country Songs,* 1.

3. James Rooney, *Bossmen: Bill Monroe and Muddy Waters,* 57.

Chapter 5. The World War II Years

1. John Woodruff Rumble, "Fred Rose and the Development of the Nashville Music Industry, 1942–1954." Rumble discusses this change in the structure of country songs in his dissertation.

Chapter 6. After the War

1. Alexander, *Our Game,* 203.

2. Ibid., 198.

3. Ibid., 206.

4. Ibid., 216.

5. Bill O'Neal, *The Pacific Coast League: 1903–1988,* 91.

6. "Fort Knox No Longer Has Exclusive on Pot of Gold; WSM, Nashville, Talent Corners a Good Chunk of It," *Variety,* Oct. 26, 1949.

Chapter 7. The Fifties

1. Jane Holtz Kay, *Asphalt Nation: How the Automobile Took over America and How We Can Take It Back,* 213, 241.
2. Alexander, *Our Game,* 220.
3. Ibid., 221.

Chapter 11. Baseball and Country Music's Troubled Times

1. Tony Pettis, "Nashville Baseball—A Deep-rooted Southern Tradition," *Nashville Banner,* May 11, 1993.
2. White, *Creating the National Pastime,* 7.
3. *From Where I Stand: The Black Experience in Country Music.* Examples of African Americans playing country music can be heard on this boxed set.

Conclusion

1. Gene Autry, with Mickey Herkowitz, *Back in the Saddle Again,* 151.
2. David Plaut, ed., *Speaking of Baseball,* 390.

Bibliographical Essay

In this book notes are only provided for direct quotes; however, a number of sources were used in compiling this information. In researching the history of baseball the following books were invaluable: *Our Game: An American Baseball History,* by Charles C. Alexander; *Creating the National Pastime: Baseball Transforms Itself, 1903–1953,* by Edward G. White; *Baseball: An Illustrated History,* by Geoffrey C. Ward and Ken Burns; and two books by David Quentin Voigt, *American Baseball,* vol. 2, *From the Commissioners to Continental Expansion* and *American Baseball,* vol. 3, *From Postwar Expansion to the Electronic Age.*

For information about Nashville baseball and the Nashville Vols, the book *Vol Feats: Records, History and Tales of the Nashville Baseball Club in the Southern Association, 1901–1950,* by Fred Russell and George Leonard, was essential. Additionally, in the Nashville Room of the Nashville Public Library I found several valuable articles, including "Base Ball" from the *Nashville Dispatch* in 1866, several articles by Fred Russell in the *Nashville Banner,* and several articles by Kay Beasley, also in the *Nashville Banner.* Also in the Nashville

Room I found Grantland Rice's article "Base Ball's Boom in Dixie," which was superb.

Books on the Pacific Coast League include *The Pacific Coast League: 1903–1988,* by Bill O'Neal; *Runs, Hits, and an Era: The Pacific Coast League, 1903–1958,* by Paul J. Zingg; and *The Angels: Los Angeles in the Pacific Coast League, 1919–1957,* by Richard E. Beverage.

For information about baseball broadcasts on the radio my most valuable source was *Going, Going, Gone! Music and Memories from Broadcast Baseball,* by Anthony DeSimone, which included a compact disc as well as booklet.

The most valuable source for general information about baseball players came from *The Baseball Encyclopedia: The Complete and Definitive Record of Major League Baseball.*

Since I have spent a lifetime in country music—working in the industry, studying it, and writing about it—it is difficult to summarize these long years of research. While doing a biography on Eddy Arnold, I talked with Mr. Arnold about baseball in Nashville and his involvement with the sport. Also, a lot of the research that went into the Eddy Arnold biography—particularly about the 1940s—became valuable and useful in writing this book. Having said all that, I find that Don C. Doyle's book *Nashville since the 1920s* is always valuable when writing about Nashville. In writing about country music I constantly refer to Charles Wolfe's *Tennessee Strings: The Story of Country Music in Tennessee* and his chapter "The Triumph of the Hills: Country Radio, 1920–1950" in *Country: The Music and the Musicians,* edited by Paul Kingsbury and Alan Axelrod, which also has valuable chapters by Edward Morris ("New, Improved, Homogenized: Country Radio since 1950") and Bill Ivey ("The Bottom Line: Business Practices that Shaped Country Music").

The book *The Stars of Country Music,* edited by Bill Malone and Judith McCulloh, was most helpful, especially the chapters on Gene Autry by Doug Green and on Vernon Dalhart by Norm Cohen. Bill Malone's work is always valuable, for this book especially *Singing Cowboys and Musical Mountaineers: Southern Culture and the Roots of Country Music* and *Country Music U.S.A.*

The best book on Jimmie Rodgers is *Jimmie Rodgers: The Life and Times of America's Blue Yodeler,* by Nolan Porterfield. A valuable source on the Opry is Chet Hagen's *Grand Ole Opry: The Complete Story of a Great American Institution and Its Stars.* And John Rumble's unpublished dissertation, "Fred Rose and the Development of the Nashville Music Industry, 1942–1954," is a treasure. Information on Roy Acuff came primarily from Elizabeth Schlappi's *Roy Acuff: The Smoky Mountain Boy,* and the information on Charley Pride's baseball career came from his autobiography, *Pride: The Charley Pride Story,* written with Jim Henderson.

For general information about the music business, I depended on Russell Sanjek's *American Popular Music and Its Business: The First Four Hundred Years,* vol. 3, *From 1900 to 1984.* A good source on country songs and artists in *Billboard* is Joel Whitburn's *Top Country Singles 1944–1988,* and for information on V-Discs there is Richard Sears's *V-Discs: A History and Discography.*

For my information on country music on television I used an unpublished study done by Ronnie Pugh and John Rumble at the Country Music Foundation as well as *The Complete Directory to Prime Time Network TV Shows: 1946–Present,* by Tim Brooks and Earle Marsh.

A valuable source discussing the role African Americans have played in country music, as well as examples of their music, is in the three CD set *From Where I Stand: The Black Experience in Country Music,* produced by the Country Music Foundation.

Information about Little League came primarily from Garry Wills's book *Certain Trumpets: The Call of Leaders.*

Bibliography

Alexander, Charles C. *Our Game: An American Baseball History*. New York: Henry Holt, 1991.

Ambrose, Stephen E. *Eisenhower: Soldier and President*. New York: Touchstone, 1990.

Angell, Roger. *The Summer Game*. New York: Penguin, 1990.

Autry, Gene, with Mickey Herkowitz. *Back in the Saddle Again*. Garden City, N.Y.: Doubleday, 1978.

Barnouw, Erik. *A Tower in Babel: A History of Broadcasting in the United States*. Vol. 1, *To 1933*. New York: Oxford University Press, 1966.

———. *The Golden Web: A History of Broadcasting in the United States*. Vol. 2, *1933 to 1953*. New York: Oxford University Press, 1968.

———. *The Image Empire: A History of Broadcasting in the United States*. Vol. 3, *From 1953*. New York: Oxford University Press, 1970.

"Base Ball." *Nashville Dispatch,* Aug. 1, 17, 18, 1866.

Baseball: Doubleheader Collection of Facts, Feats and Firsts. Comp. *The Sporting News* editors. New York: Galahad Books, 1993.

Baseball Encyclopedia: The Complete and Definitive Record of Major League Baseball. 10th ed. New York: Macmillan, 1996.

Beasley, Kay. "Out to the Baseball Game at Old Sulphur Dell." *Nashville Banner,* Apr. 23, 1986.

———. "Vols' Golden Era Began in 1939." *Nashville Banner,* July 5, 1989.

Beverage, Richard E. *The Angels: Los Angeles in the Pacific Coast League, 1919–1957.* Placentia, Calif.: Deacon Press, 1981.

Bjarkman, Peter C., ed. *Encyclopedia of Major League Baseball Team Histories: National League.* Westport, Conn.: Meckler, 1991.

Brooks, Tim, and Earle Marsh. *The Complete Directory to Prime Time Network TV Shows: 1946–Present.* New York: Ballantine, 1988.

Bufwack, Mary, and Robert K. Oermann. *Finding Her Voice: The Saga of Women in Country Music.* New York: Crown, 1993.

"Bull Market in Corn." *Time,* Oct. 4, 1943.

Burk, Robert F. *Never Just a Game: Players, Owners, and American Baseball to 1920.* Chapel Hill: University of North Carolina Press, 1995.

Burt, Jesse C. *Nashville: Its Life and Times.* Nashville: Tennessee Book Co., 1959.

Carney, George O. *Popular Culture: A Geographical Interpretation.* Lanham, Md.: Rowman and Littlefield, 19XX.

Carr, Patrick, ed. *The Illustrated History of Country Music.* From the editors of *Country Music Magazine.* New York: Random House/Times Books, 1996.

Chadwick, Bruce. *Baseball's Hometown Teams: The Story of the Minor Leagues.* New York: Abbeville Press, 1994.

Churchill, Allen. "Tin Pan Alley's Git-Tar Blues." *New York Times Magazine,* July 15, 1951.

Conot, Robert. *A Streak of Luck.* New York: Seaview Books, 1979.

Coontz, Stephanie. *The Way We Never Were: American Families and the Nostalgia Trap.* New York: Basic Books, 1992.

"Corn of Plenty." *Newsweek,* June 13, 1949.

"Country Music Goes to Town." *Mademoiselle,* April 1948.

"Country Music Is Big Business, and Nashville Is Its Detroit." *Newsweek,* Aug. 11, 1952.

"Country Music Snaps Its Regional Bounds." *Business Week,* Mar. 19, 1966.

"Country Music: The Nashville Sound." *Time,* Nov. 17, 1964.

"Country Musicians Fiddle Up Roaring Business." *Life,* Nov. 19, 1956.

Creamer, Robert W. *Stengel: His Life and Times.* Lincoln: University of Nebraska Press, 1996.

Crowell, Thomas Y. *Stephen Foster, America's Troubadour.* New York: Thomas Y. Crowell Co., 1934, 1953.

Davis, Louise Littleton. *Nashville Tales.* Gretna, Ga.: Pelica, 1982.

DeSimone, Anthony. *Going, Going, Gone! Music and Memories from Broadcast Baseball.* With compact disc. New York: Friedman/Fairfax, 1994.

Dewey, Donald, and Nicholas Acocella. *Encyclopedia of Major League Baseball Teams.* New York: HarperCollins, 1993.

———. *The Biographical History of Baseball.* New York: Carroll and Graf Publishers, 1995.

DiMaggio, Dom, and Bill Gilbert. *Real Grass, Real Heroes.* New York: Zebra, 1990.

Doyle, Don C. *Nashville since the 1920s.* Knoxville: University of Tennessee Press, 1985.

———. *New Men, New Cities, New South: Atlanta, Nashville, Charleston, Mobile, 1860–1910.* Chapel Hill: University of North Carolina Press, 1990.

Duff, Morris. "Make Way for the Country Sound." *Toronto Daily Star,* Mar. 21, 1964.

Eddy, Don. "Hillbilly Heaven." *American Magazine,* Mar. 1952.

Erickson, Hal. *Baseball in the Movies: A Comprehensive Reference, 1915–1991.* Jefferson, N.C.: McFarland, 1992.

Escott, Colin, with George Merritt and William MacEwen. *Hank Williams: The Biography.* Boston: Little, Brown, 1994.

Falkner, David. *Great Time Coming: The Life of Jackie Robinson, from Baseball to Birmingham.* New York: Simon and Schuster, 1995.

———. *The Last Hero: The Life of Mickey Mantle.* New York: Simon and Schuster, 1995.

Feinstein, John. *Play Ball: The Life and Troubled Times of Major League Baseball.* New York: Villard, 1993.

Filichia, Peter. *Professional Baseball Franchises: From the Abbeville Athletics to the Zanesville Indians.* New York: Facts on File, 1993.

Fimrite, Ron. *The World Series: A History of Baseball's Fall Classic.* Birmingham, Ala.: Oxmoor House, 1993.

"First Baseball Game Here Was in Late Sixties: Nashvillians Learned How to Play It From Herman Sandhouse." *Nashville Banner,* Oct. 30, 1932.

"Fort Knox No Longer Has Exclusive on Pot of Gold; WSM, Nashville, Talent Corners a Good Chunk of It." *Variety,* Oct. 26, 1949.

Founttain, Charles. *Sportswriter: The Life and Times of*

Grantland Rice. New York: Oxford University Press, 1995.

From Where I Stand: The Black Experience in Country Music. Produced by the Country Music Foundation. Warner Brothers, 1998. 3 compact discs.

Gentry, Linnell. *A History and Encyclopedia of Country, Western, and Gospel Music.* Nashville: Clairmont, 1969.

"The Gold Guitars." *Newsweek,* Apr. 4, 1966.

Goldstein, Warren. *Playing for Keeps: A History of Early Baseball.* Ithaca, N.Y.: Cornell University Press, 1989.

Goodwin, Doris Kearns. *No Ordinary Time: Franklin and Eleanor Roosevelt: The Home Front in World War II.* New York: Touchstone, 1994.

Graebner, William S. *The Age of Doubt: American Thought and Culture in the 1940s.* Boston: Twyane, 1991.

Greatest Baseball Players of All Time. Lincolnwood, Ill.: Publications, International, Ltd, 1990.

Green, Douglas B. *Country Roots: The Origins of Country Music.* New York: Hawthorn, 1976.

Gregory, Robert. *Diz: The Story of Dizzy Dean and Baseball during the Great Depression.* New York: Penguin, 1992.

Guralnick, Peter. *Last Train to Memphis: The Rise of Elvis Presley.* Boston: Little, Brown, 1994.

Hagen, Chet. *Grand Ole Opry: The Complete Story of a Great American Institution and Its Stars.* New York: Owl, 1989.

Halberstam, David. *October 1964.* New York: Villard, 1994.

Hall, Alvin L., ed. *Cooperstown.* Westport, Conn.: Meckler, 1991.

Hall, Wade. *Hell Bent for Music: Pee Wee King.* Lexington: University of Kentucky Press, 1996.

Harris, Roy. "Folk Songs." *House and Garden,* Dec. 1954.

Heide, R., and J. Gilman. *Home Front America: Popular*

Culture of the World War II Era. San Francisco: Chronicle, 1995.

Helyar, John. *Lords of the Realm: The Real History of Baseball.* New York: Villard, 1994.

Hemphill, Paul. *The Nashville Sound: Bright Lights and Country Music.* New York: Simon and Schuster, 1970.

"Hoedown on a Harpsichord." *Time,* Nov. 14, 1960.

Horstman, Dorothy. *Sing Your Heart Out, Country Boy: Classic Country Songs and Their Inside Stories by the People Who Wrote Them.* New York: E. P. Dutton, 1975.

Ivey, Bill. "The Bottom Line: Business Practices that Shaped Country Music." In *Country: The Music and the Musicians,* edited by Paul Kingsbury and Alan Axelrod. New York: Abbeville Press, 1988.

Jackson, Kenneth T. *Crabgrass Frontier: The Suburbanization of the United States.* New York: Oxford University Press, 1985.

James, Bill. *The Politics of Glory: How Baseball's Hall of Fame Really Works.* New York: Macmillan, 1994.

Jarman, Rufus. "Country Music Goes to Town." *Nation's Business,* Feb. 1953.

Johnson, Lloyd. *Baseball's Dream Teams: The Greatest Major League Players Decade by Decade.* Avenel, N.J.: Crescent Books, 1990.

Joyce, Gare. *The Only Ticket Off the Island.* Toronto: Lester and Orpen Dennys, 1990.

Kahn, Roger. *The Era 1947–1957: When the Yankees, The Giants, and the Dodgers Ruled the World.* New York: Ticknor and Fields, 1993.

Kay, Jane Holtz. *Asphalt Nation: How the Automobile Took Over America and How We Can Take It Back.* New York: Crown, 1997.

King, Larry L. "Inside Grand Ole Opry." *Reader's Digest,* July 1968; condensed from *Harper's,* July 1968.

King, Nelson. "Hillbilly Music Leaves the Hills." *Good Housekeeping,* June 1954.

Kingsbury, Paul. *The Grand Ole Opry History of Country Music: Seventy Years of the Songs, the Stars, and the Stories.* New York: Villard, 1995.

————, ed. *The Country Music Reader.* Nashville: Vanderbilt University Press, 1996.

Kingsbury, Paul, and Alan Axelrod, eds. *Country: The Music and the Musicians.* New York: Abbeville Press, 1988.

Kittsinger, Otto. Liner notes for *Pee Wee King & the Golden West Cowboys.* Hambergen, Germany: Bear Family Records, 1992.

Langdon, Philip. *A Better Place to Live: Reshaping the American Suburb.* Amherst: University of Massachusetts Press, 1994.

LeBlanc, Michael L. *Hotdogs, Heroes and Hooligans: The Story of Baseball's Major League Teams.* Detroit: Visible Ink Press, 1994.

Lewis, Tom. *Divided Highways: Building the Interstate Highways, Transforming American Life.* New York: Viking, 1997.

Lieberson, Goddard. "Country Sweeps the Country." *New York Times Magazine,* July 28, 1957.

Malone, Bill. *Country Music U.S.A.* Austin: University of Texas Press, 1968.

————. *Singing Cowboys and Musical Mountaineers: Southern Culture and the Roots of Country Music.* Athens: University of Georgia Press, 1993.

Malone, Bill C., and Judith McCulloh, eds. *The Stars of Country Music.* Urbana: University of Illinois Press, 1975.

Mantle, Mickey, and M. Herskowitz. *All My Octobers.* New York: HarperCollins, 1994.

Marek, Richard. "Country Music, Nashville Style." *Mc-Call's,* April 1961.

McCloud, Barry. *Definitive Country: The Ultimate Encyclopedia of Country Music and Its Performers.* New York: Perigree, 1995.

McCue, Andy. *Baseball by the Books.* Dubuque, Iowa: Wm. C. Brown, 1991.

McElvaine, Robert S. *The Great Depression: America 1929–1941.* New York: Times, 1984.

Mercurio, John A. *Record Profiles of Baseball's Hall of Famers.* New York: Harper and Row, 1990.

Monroe, Bill. *Bill Monroe's Blue Grass Country Songs.* Beverly Hills, Calif.: Bill Monroe Music, 1950.

Morris, Edward. "New, Improved, Homogenized: Country Radio since 1950." In *Country: The Music and the Musicians,* edited by Paul Kingsbury and Alan Axelrod. New York: Abbeville Press, 1988.

Mote, James. *Everything Baseball.* New York: Prentice-Hall, 1989.

Murdock, Eugene. *Baseball between the Wars.* Westport, Conn.: Meckler, 1992.

Nash, Alanna. *Behind Closed Doors: Talking with the Legends of Country Music.* New York: Alfred A. Knopf, 1988.

Neft, David S., and Richard M. Cohen. *The Sports Encyclopedia: Baseball.* New York: St. Martin's Press, 1995.

Oermann, Robert. *America's Music: The Roots of Country.* Atlanta: Turner Publisher, 1996.

O'Neal, Bill. *The Pacific Coast League: 1903–1988.* Austin, Tex.: Eakin Press, 1990.

Palmer, Pete, and John Thorn, eds. *The Baseball Record Book.* New York: Simon and Schuster, 1991.

Pettis, Tony. "Nashville Baseball—A Deep-rooted Southern Tradition." *Nashville Banner,* May 11, 1993.

"Pistol Packin' Mama." *Life,* Oct. 11, 1943.

Plaut, David, ed. *Speaking of Baseball.* Philadelphia: Running Press 1993.

Porterfield, Nolan. *Jimmie Rodgers: The Life and Times of America's Blue Yodeler.* Urbana: University of Illinois Press, 1979.

Portis, Charles. "That New Sound from Nashville." *Saturday Evening Post,* Feb. 12, 1966.

Pride, Charley, with Jim Henderson. *Pride: The Charley Pride Story.* New York: William Morrow, 1994.

Pugh, Ronnie. *Ernest Tubb: Texas Troubadour.* Durham, N.C.: Duke University Press, 1996.

Reichler, Joseph L. *The Baseball Record Companion: A Miscellaneous Compendium of Great Feats, Strange Facts, and Other Assorted Figures.* New York: Macmillan, 1987.

Reidenbaugh, Lowell, and Joe Hoppel. *Baseball's Hall of Fame: Cooperstown, Where the Legends Live Forever.* Comp. The Sporting News editors. New York: Crescent, 1993.

Rice, Grantland. "Base Ball's Boom in Dixie." *Taylor Trotwood Magazine,* May 1910.

Ritter, Lawrence. *The Glory of Their Times: The Story of the Early Days of Baseball Told by the Men Who Played It.* New York: Quill, 1976.

Ritter, Lawrence, and Donald Honig. *The Image of Their Greatness.* New York: Crown, 1984.

Rooney, James. *Bossmen: Bill Monroe and Muddy Waters.* New York: Dial Press, 1971.

Rosenberg, Neil V. *Bluegrass: A History.* Urbana: University of Illinois Press, 1985.

Ruck, Rob. *The Tropic of Baseball: Baseball in the Dominican Republic.* Westport, Conn.: Meckler, 1991.

Rumble, John Woodruff. "Fred Rose and the Development of the Nashville Music Industry, 1942–1954." Ph.D. diss., Vanderbilt University, 1980. Ann Arbor, Mich.: University Microfilms International.

Russell, Fred. "Memories Linger of Nashville's Unique Ball Park, Sulphur Dell." *Nashville Banner,* Mar. 18, 1988.

———. "A Nod to Sulphur Dell Alumni Who Thrived in Major Leagues." *Nashville Banner,* Aug. 16, 1990.

Russell, Fred, and George Leonard. *Vol Feats: Records, History and Tales of the Nashville Baseball Club in the Southern Association, 1901–1950.* Nashville: Nashville Banner, 1950.

Samuelson, Robert J. *The Good Life and Its Discontents: The American Dream in the Age of Entitlement, 1945–1995.* New York: Times Books/Random House, 1995.

Sanjek, Russell. *American Popular Music and Its Business: The First Four Hundred Years.* Vol. 3, *From 1900 to 1984.* New York: Oxford University Press, 1988.

Scherman, Robert. "Hillbilly Phenomenon." *Christian Science Monitor,* Mar. 13, 1948.

Schlappi, Elizabeth. *Roy Acuff: The Smoky Mountain Boy.* Gretna, Ga.: Pelican Publishing Company, 1993.

Sears, Richard S. *V-Discs: A History and Discography.* Westport, Conn.: Greenwood Press, 1980.

Sharp, Cecil J., and Olive Dame Campbell. *English Folk Songs from the Southern Appalachians.* New York: Oxford University Press, 1966.

Shatzkin, Mike. *The Ballplayers: Baseball's Ultimate Biographical Reference.* New York: Arbor House/William Morrow, 1990.

Shelton, Robert, and Burt Goldblatt. *The Country Music Story.* New York: Bobbs-Merrill, 1966.

Smith, Myron J. *Baseball: A Comprehensive Bibliography.* Jefferson, N.C.: McFarland, 1993.

Smith, Ron. *The Sporting News Chronicle of Baseball.* New York: BDD Illustrated Books, 1993.

"Songs from Texas." *Time,* Mar. 24, 1941.

Staten, Vince. *Ol' Diz: A Biography of Dizzy Dean.* New York: HarperCollins, 1992.

Stone, Jack. "Millions in Music—Hillbillies in Clover." *American Weekly,* Feb. 6, 1949.

"Strictly by Ear." *Time,* Feb. 11, 1946.

Sugar, Bert Randolph. *Baseball's Fifty Greatest Games.* North Dighton, Mass.: JG Press/World Publications, 1994.

Sullivan, Dean A., ed. *Early Innings: A Documentary History of Baseball, 1825–1908.* Lincoln: University of Nebraska Press, 1995.

Teeter, H. B. "Nashville, Broadway of Country Music." *Coronet,* Aug. 1952.

Thorn, John, and Peter Palmer, eds. *Total Baseball.* 4th ed. New York: Viking, 1995.

Tichi, Cecelia. *High Lonesome: The American Culture of Country Music.* Chapel Hill: University of North Carolina Press, 1994.

Tilley, Nannie M. *The R. J. Reynolds Tobacco Company.* Chapel Hill: University of North Carolina Press, 1985.

Tosches, Nick. *Country: The Biggest Music in America.* New York: Delta, 1977.

Turner, Frederick. *When the Boys Came Back: Baseball and 1946.* New York: Henry Holt, 1996.

Voigt, David Quentin. *American Baseball.* Vol. 1, *From*

Gentleman's Sport to the Commissioner System. University Park: Pennsylvania State University Press, 1983.

———. *American Baseball.* Vol. 2, *From the Commissioners to Continental Expansion.* University Park: Pennsylvania State University Press, 1983.

———. *American Baseball.* Vol. 3, *From Postwar Expansion to the Electronic Age.* University Park: Pennsylvania State University Press, 1983.

Waldron, Eli. "Country Music: The Squaya Dansu from Nashville." *The Reporter,* June 2, 1955.

Ward, Geoffrey, and Ken Burns. *Baseball: An Illustrated History.* New York: Knopf, 1994.

Webb, Ned C. "The Travails of a Batboy: Or, What It Was Like before All Baseball Players Were Superstars." *Nashville Tennessean,* Dec. 1977.

Weiss, Michael J. *The Clustering of America: A Vivid Portrait of the Nation's Forty Neighborhood Types—Their Values, Lifestyles and Eccentricities.* New York: Harper and Row, 1988.

Whitburn, Joel. *Top Country Singles, 1944–1988.* Menomonee Falls, Wisc.: Record Research Inc., 1989.

———. *Top Pop Singles, 1955–1990.* Menomonee Falls, Wisc.: Record Research Inc, 1991.

White, G. Edward. *Creating the National Pastime: Baseball Transforms Itself, 1903–1953.* Princeton, N.J.: Princeton University Press, 1996.

Williams, Peter. *When the Giants Were Giants: Bill Terry and the Golden Age of New York Baseball.* Chapel Hill, N.C.: Algonquin, 1994.

Williams, Roger. *Sing a Sad Song: The Life of Hank Williams.* New York: Ballantine, 1973.

Wills, Garry. *Certain Trumpets: The Call of Leaders.* New York: Simon and Schuster, 1994.

Wolfe, Charles K. *Tennesse Strings: The Story of Country Music in Tennessee.* Knoxville: University of Tennessee Press, 1977.

———. "The Triumph of the Hills: Country Radio, 1920–1950." In *Country: The Music and the Musicians,* edited by Paul Kingsbury and Alan Axelrod. New York: Abbeville Press, 1988.

Zingg, Paul J. *Runs, Hits, and an Era: The Pacific Coast League, 1903–1958.* Urbana: University of Illinois Press, 1994.

Zolotow, Maurice. "Hillbilly Boom." *Saturday Evening Post,* Feb. 12, 1944.

Zoss, Joel, and John S. Bowen. *The History of Major League Baseball.* Avenel, N.J.: Crescent Books, 1992.

Index

Index

Index

MacPhail, Larry, 77
Major League Players Association, 5
Malmud, Bernard, 70
Mantle, Mickey, 33, 95, 120, 132, 133
Marion, Marty, 67, 76
Martin, Billy, 83
Martin, Pepper, 57
Martin, Terry, 76
Marvin, Dick, 41
Mathewson, Christy, 48
Matthews, Eddie, 120
Maynardville, Tennessee, 54
Mays, Willie, 95, 120, 124
McEntire, Reba, 6
McGee, Sam and Kirk, 41, 62
McGheehan, W. B., 16
McGraw, John, 49
McGwire, Mark, 144
McNamee, Graham, 16
Medwick, Joe, 58
Melody Ranch, 57, 62
Memphis, 40, 45, 124
"Memphis Blues," 52
Memphis Chicks, 70, 80
Memphis Red Sox, 123, 124
Mercury Records, 128
Meusel, Bob, 16, 23
"Mexican Joe," 96
Miami, 140
Michigan, 8
Mid-Day Merry-Go Round, 18, 54
Midwestern Hayride, 86, 104
Miles Laboratories, 17
Miller, Glenn, 72
Miller, Marvin, 5

Miller, Roger, 113
Milwaukee, 97, 121
Minnesota Twins, 121
Mississippi, 133
Mississippi Sheiks, 131
Missoula (Montana) Timber-jacks, 124
Missouri Mountaineers, The, 62
Mize, Johnny, 68
Mobile, Alabama, 32
Mocoton Tonic, 54
Monday Night Football, 136
Monroe, Bill, 55, 56, 62, 73, 87
Montana, 125
Monterrey, Mexico, 143
Montgomery, Alabama, 40
Montreal Royals, 77
Moody, Clyde, 73
Moore, Terry, 67, 68
Moore, Wilcy, 23
Murderer's Row, 23
Murfreesboro, Tennessee, 16
Musial, Stan, 67, 68, 76, 120
Music City U.S.A., 41, 95
Music Row, 128, 140
Mutual Broadcasting System, 18, 102
"My Old Kentucky Home," 10

Nashville, 4, 7, 16, 17, 34, 35, 38, 39, 40, 43, 44, 49, 57, 58, 59, 60, 61, 65, 67, 68, 70, 72, 80, 87, 89, 95, 96, 97, 110, 111, 112, 125, 126, 127, 128, 136, 140, 142
Nashville Banner, 43
Nashville Dispatch, 38

176

A RAY AND PAT BROWNE BOOK

Series Editors
Ray B. Browne and Pat Browne

Baseball and Country Music
Don Cusic

The Essential Guide to Werewolf Literature
Brian J. Frost